Bond Assessment Papers

Fourth papers in Non-verbal Reasoning

Alison Primrose

Paper 1

Which shape is most similar to the shapes in the group on the left? Circle the letter.

Example

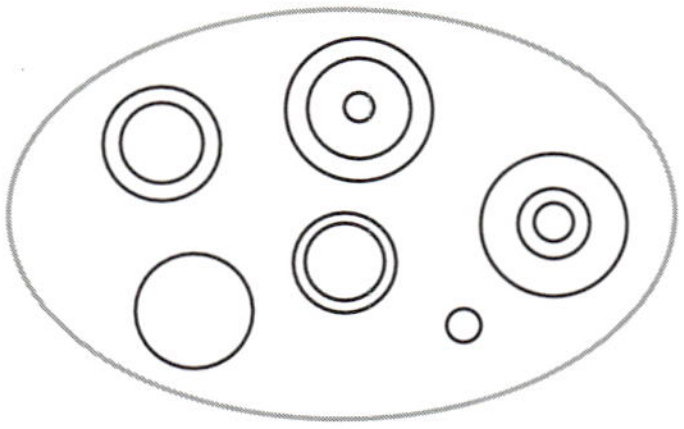

a b c d e

1

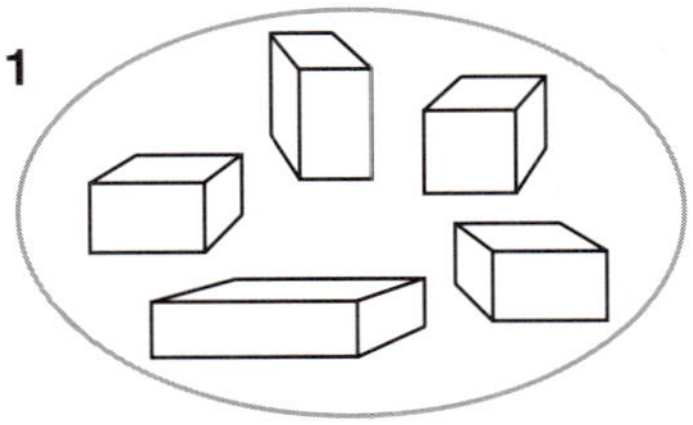

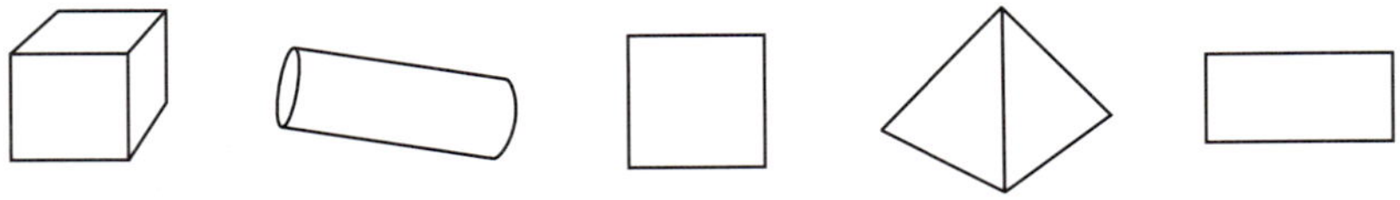

a b c d e

2

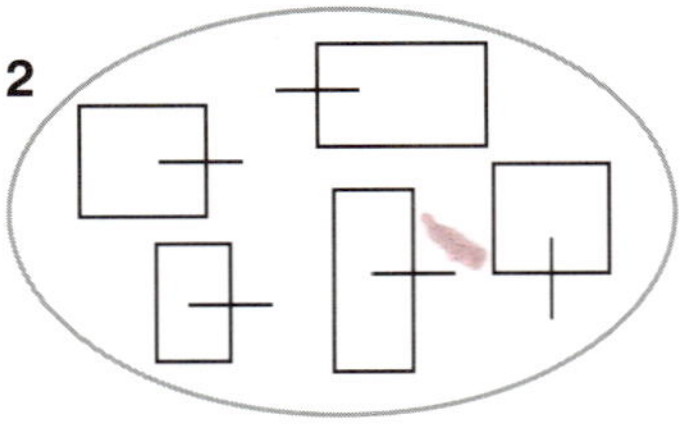

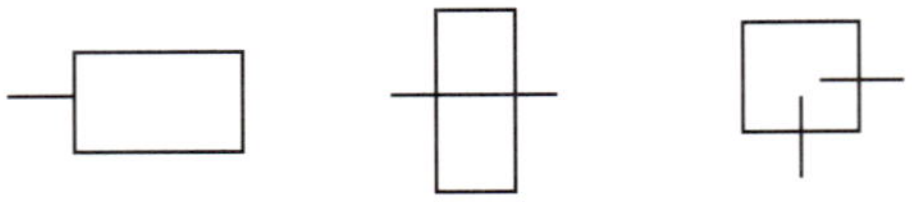

a b c d e

3

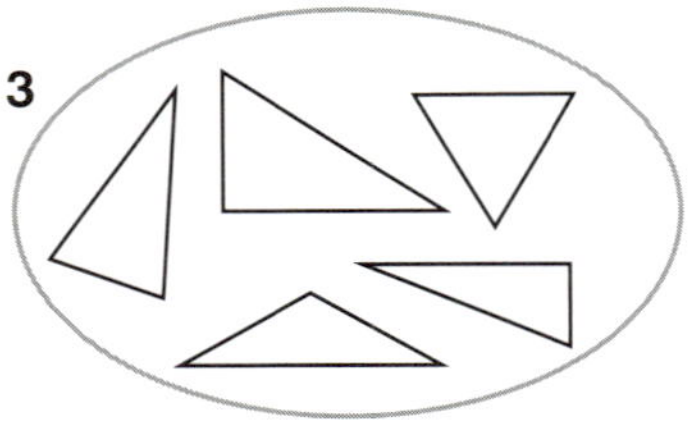

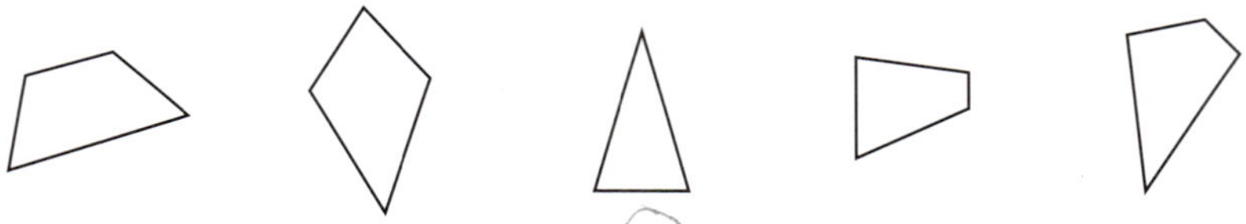

a b c d e

4

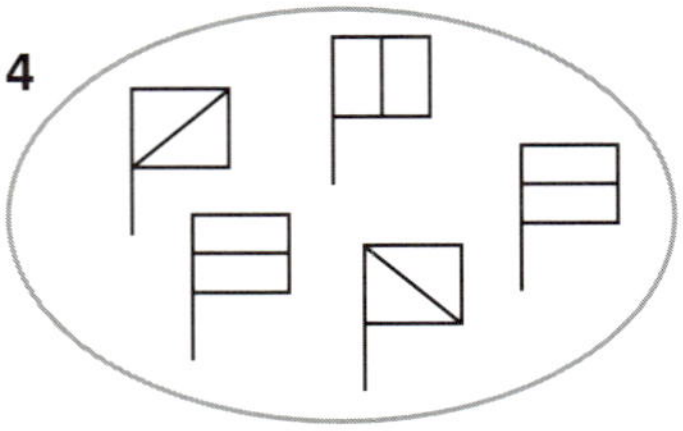

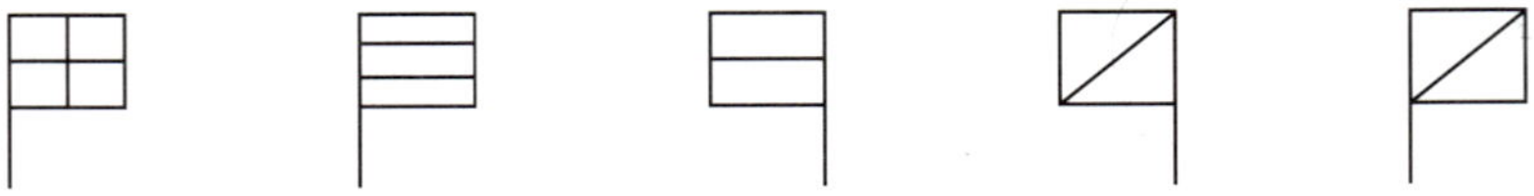

a b c d e

5

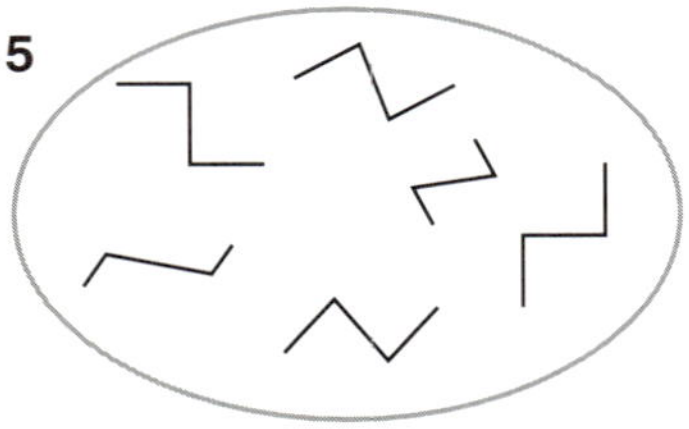

a b c d e

6

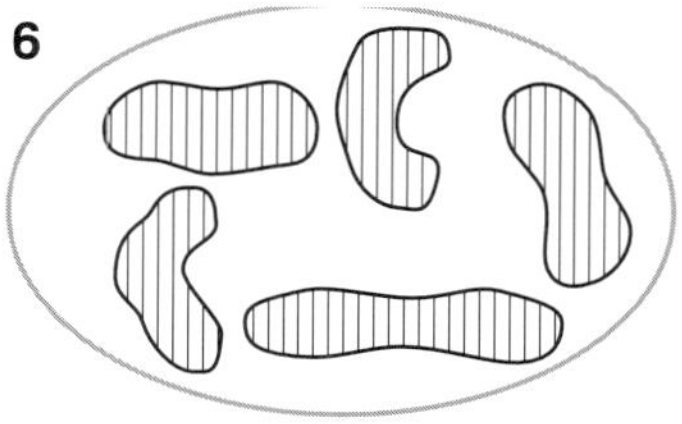

a **b** **c** **d** **e**

7

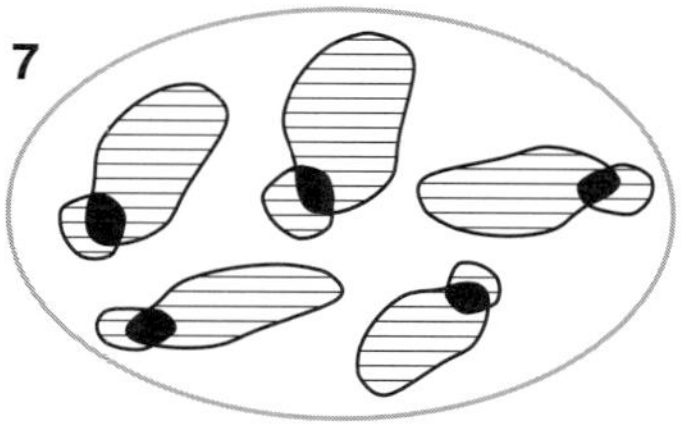

a **b** **c** **d** **e**

8

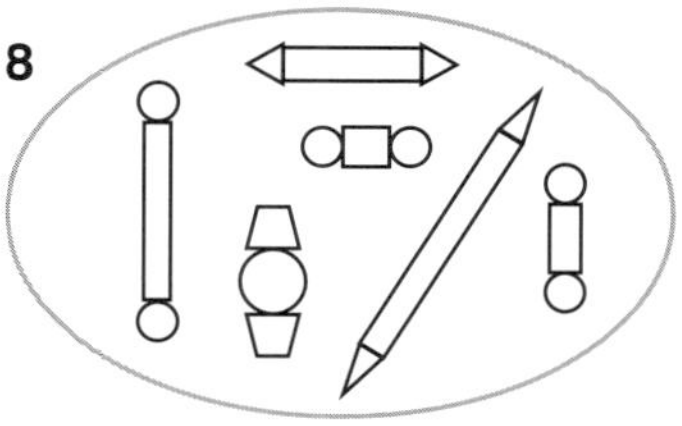

a **b** **c** **d** **e**

9

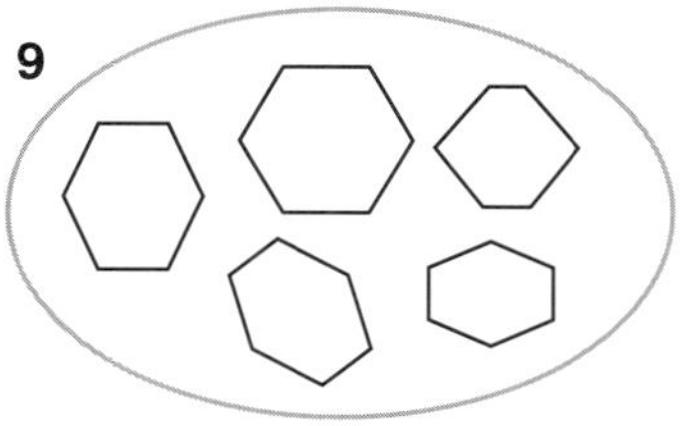

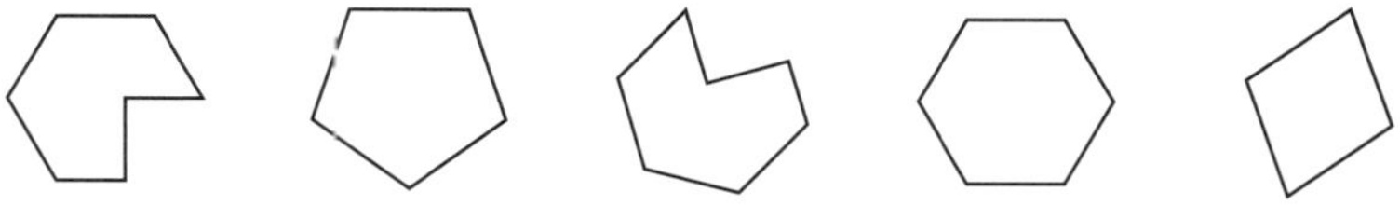

a **b** **c** **d** **e**

10

a **b** **c** **d** **e**

11

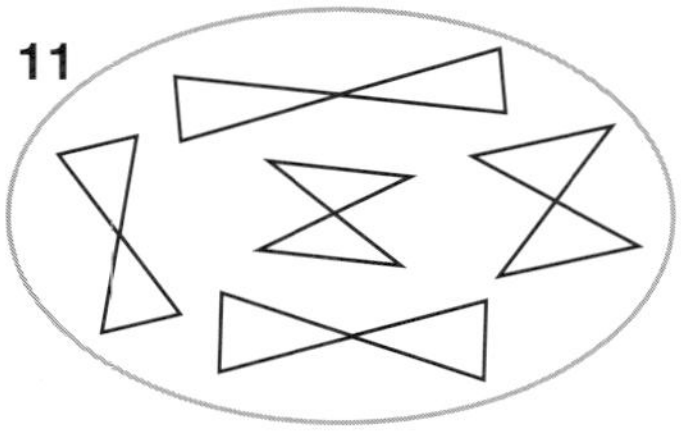

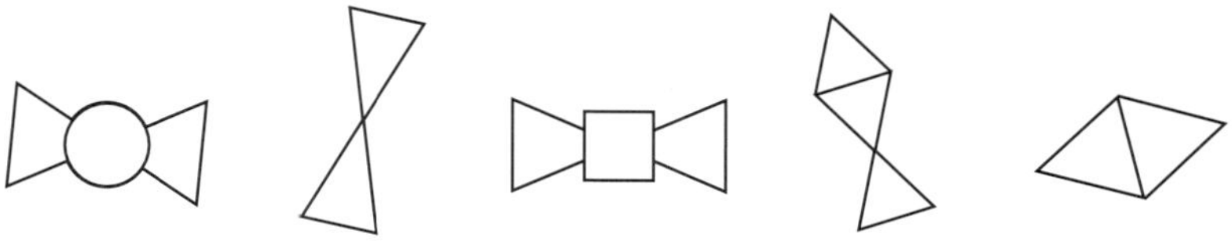

a **b** **c** **d** **e**

12

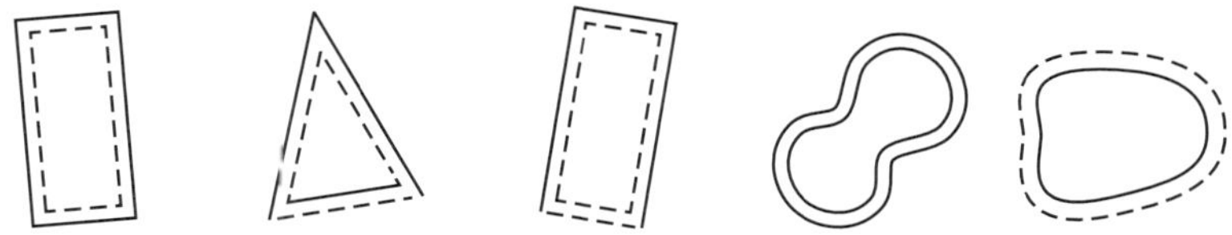

a **b** **c** **d** **e**

In which larger shape or pattern is the smaller shape hidden? Circle the letter.

Example

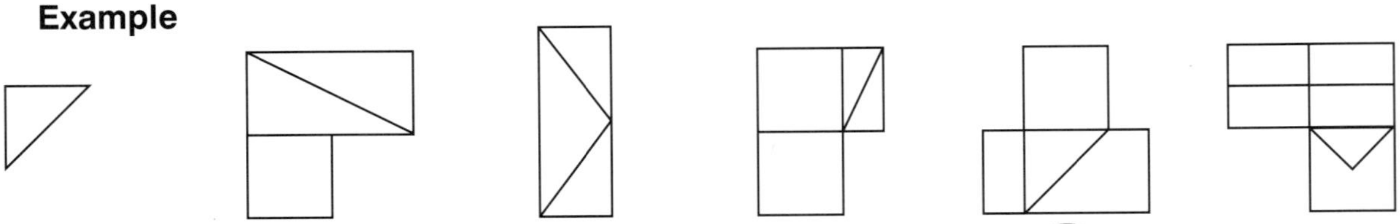

a b c d e

13

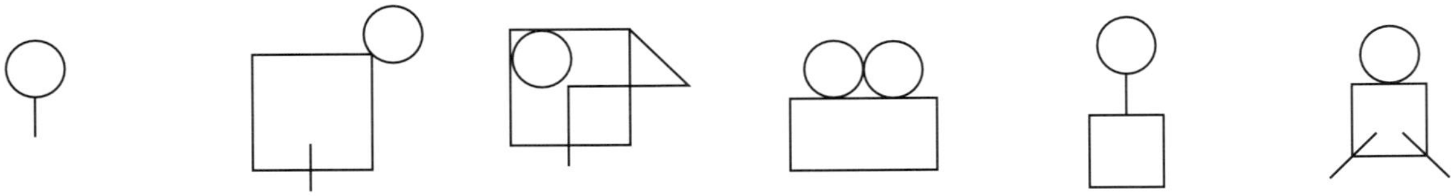

a b c d e

14

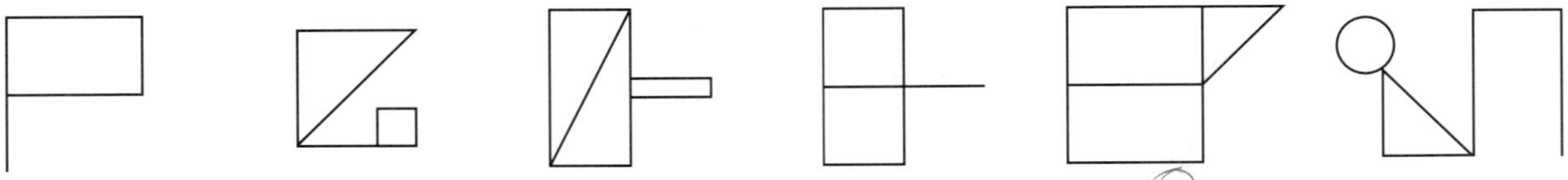

a b c d e

15

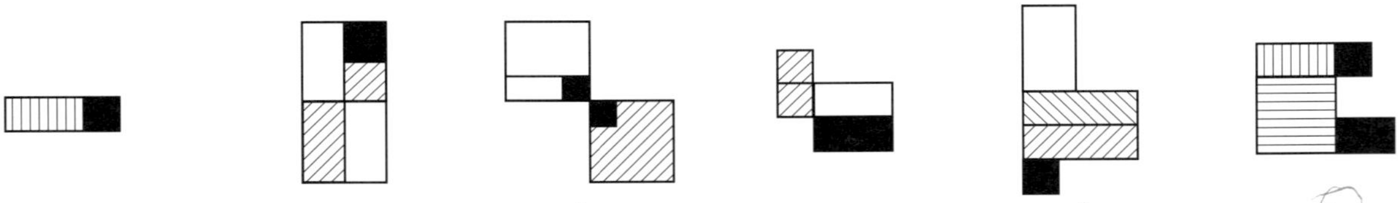

a b c d e

16

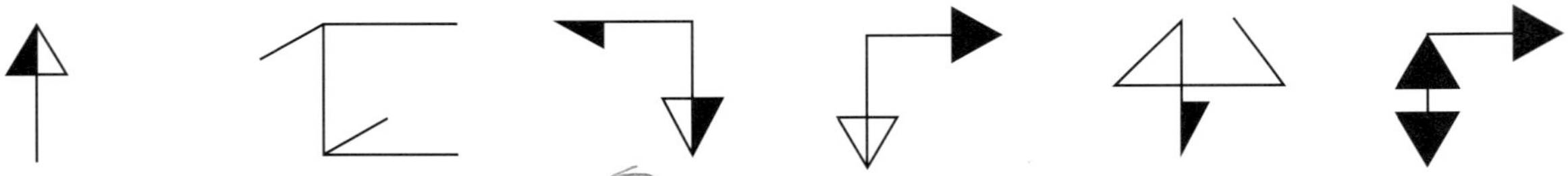

a b c d e

17

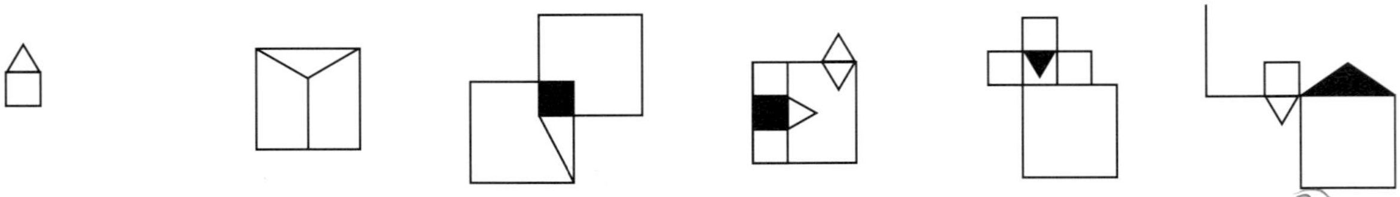

a b c d e

18

a b c d e

Find the shape or pattern which completes the second pair in the same way as the first pair. Circle the letter.

Example

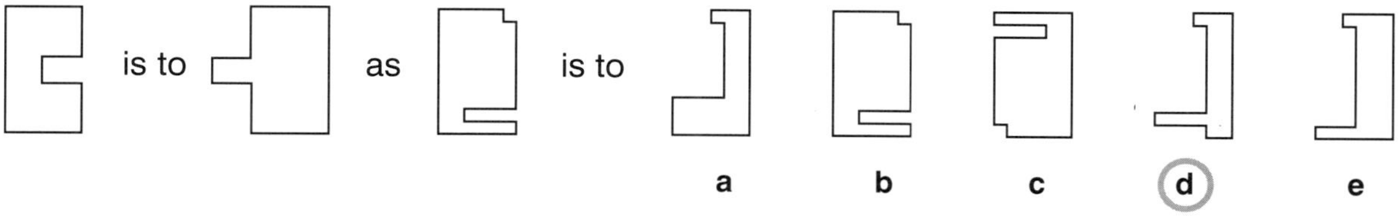

19

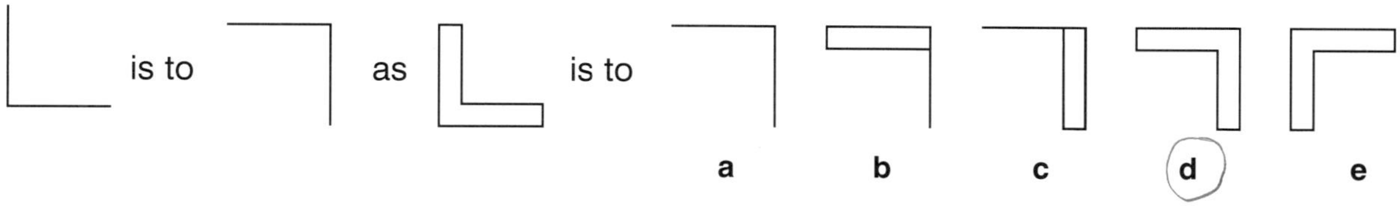

20

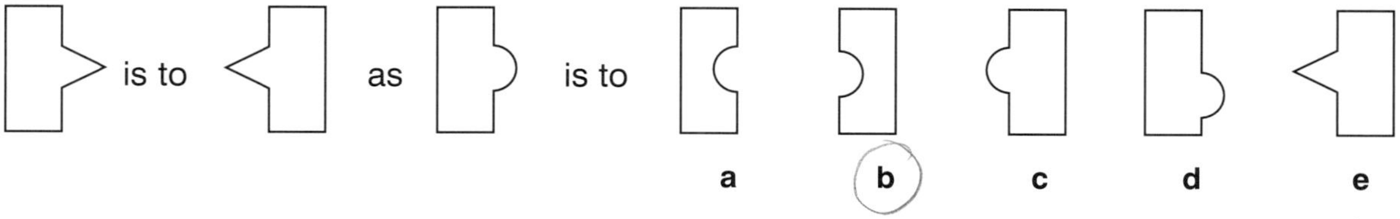

21

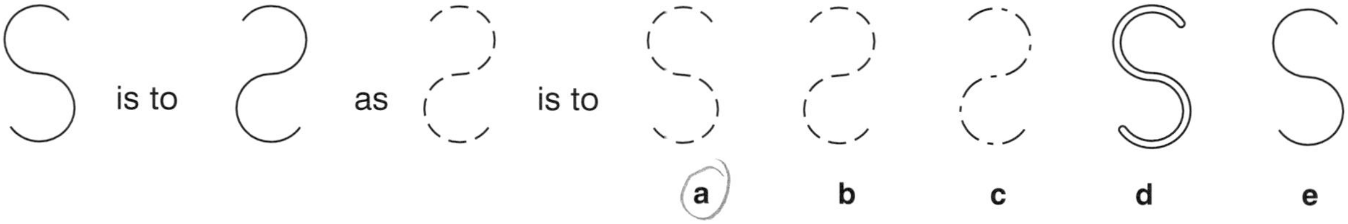

22

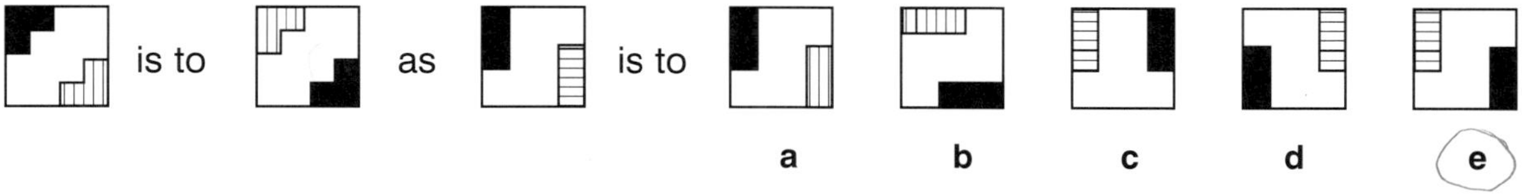

23

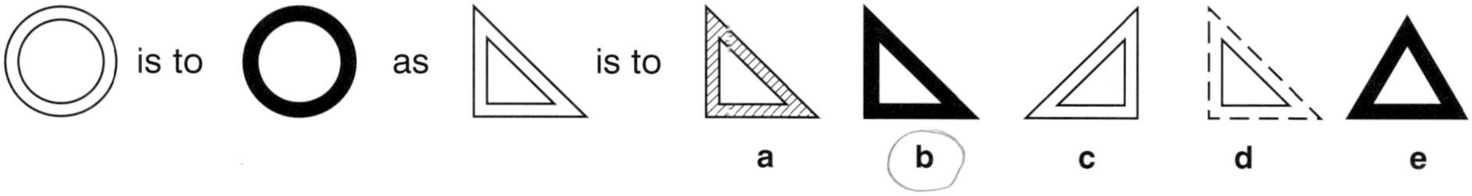

24

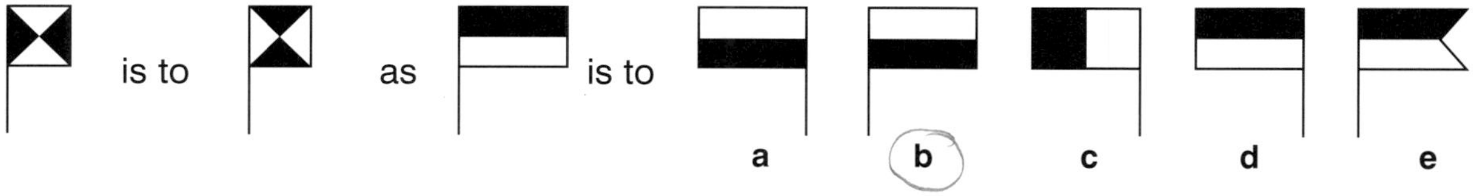

25

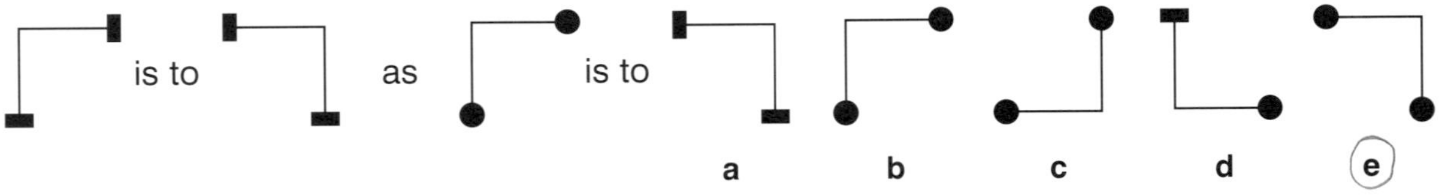

26

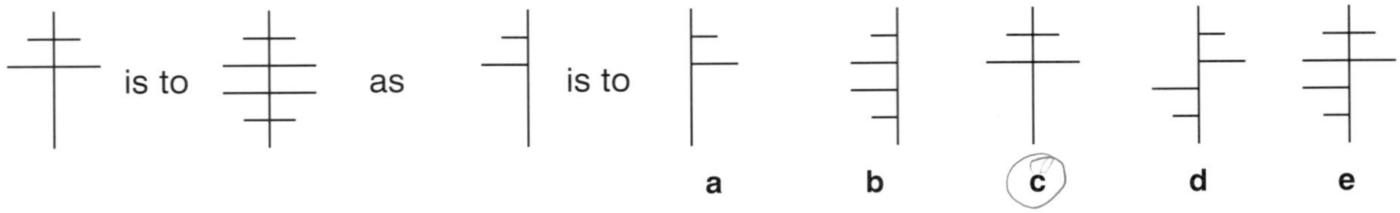

27

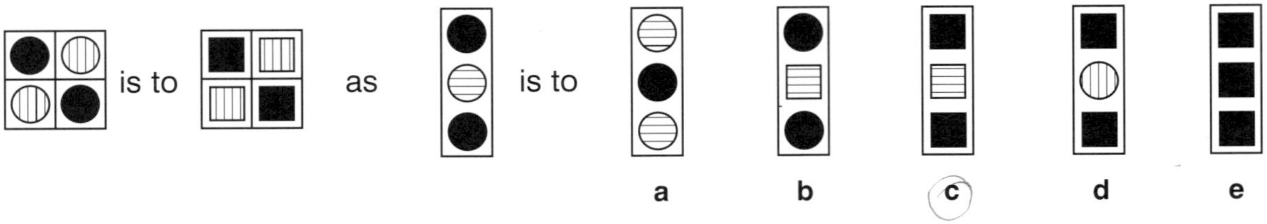

28

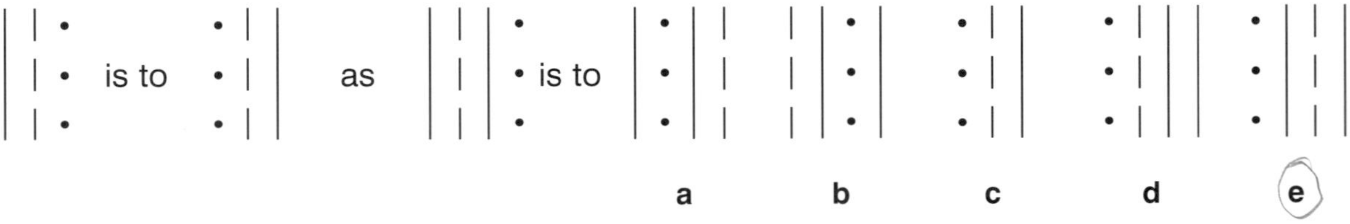

29

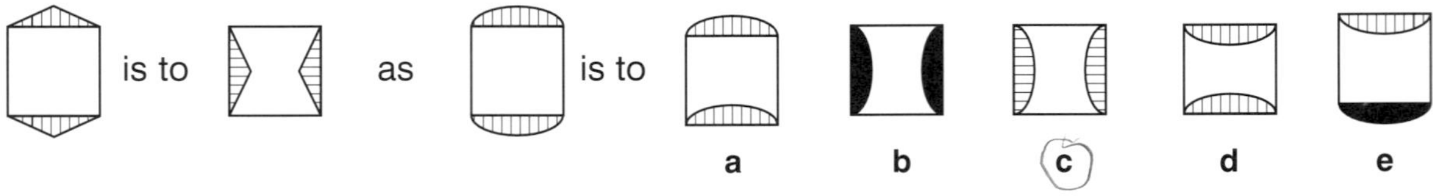

30

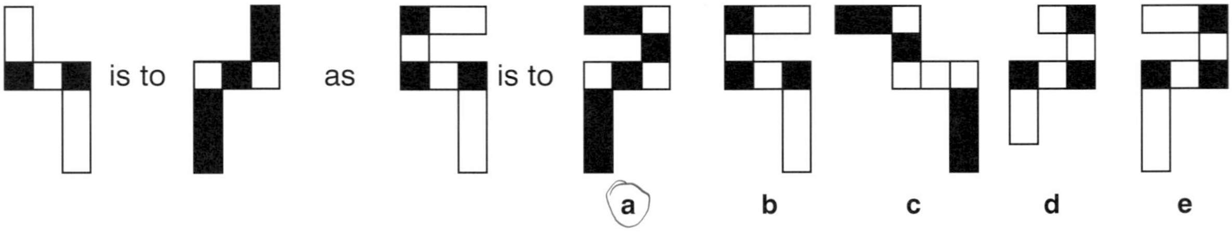

Find the shape or pattern which completes or continues the given series. Circle the letter.

Example

a b c d e

31

a b c d e

32

a b c d e

33

a b c d e

34

a b c d e

35

a b c d e

36

a b c d e

37

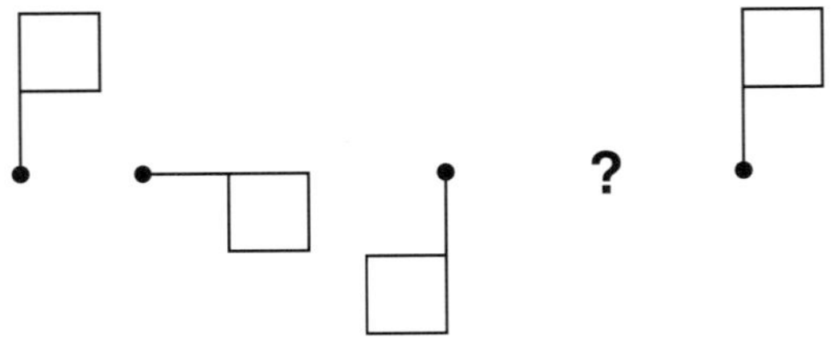

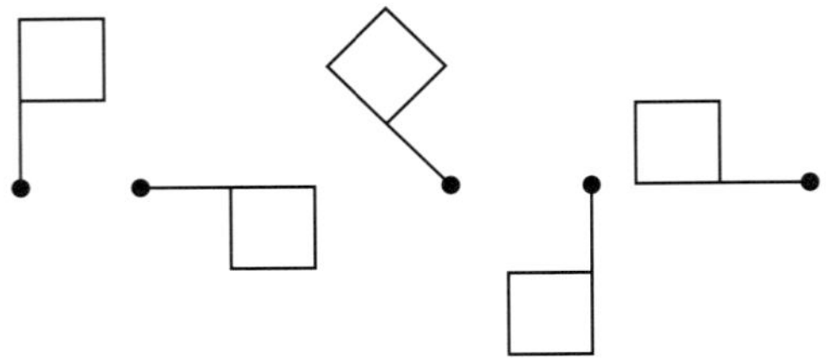

a b c d e

38

a b c d e

39

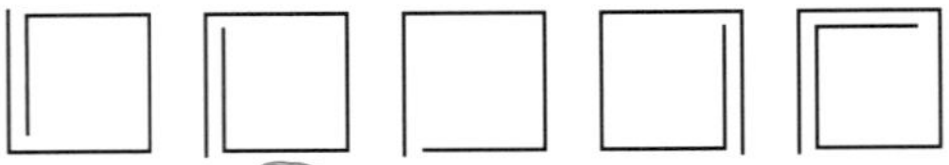

a b c d e

40

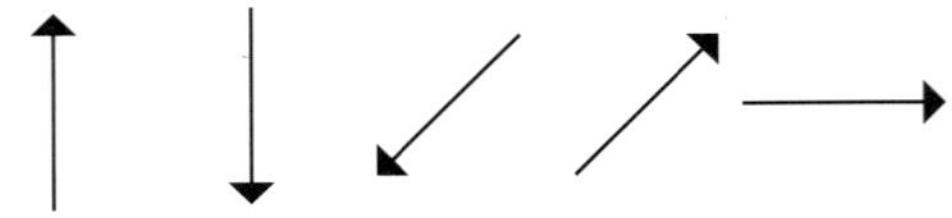

a b c d e

41

a b c d e

42

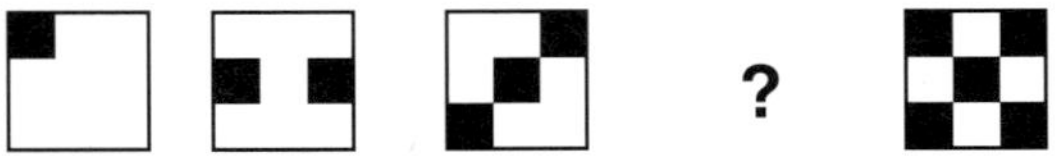

a b c d e

Look carefully at the shapes and codes given.
Select the code which matches the shape given at the end of each line.

Example

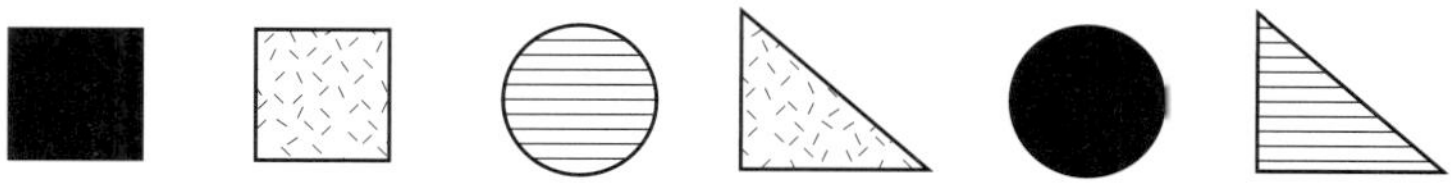

AX AY BZ CY BX ?

AY	AX	CZ	BZ	BY
a	b	c	d	e

43

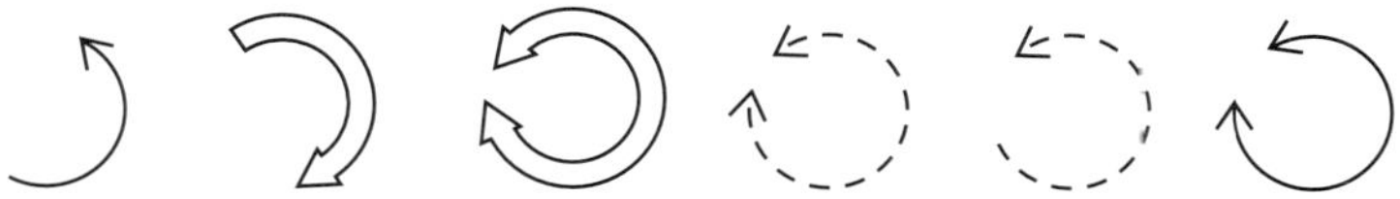

LF MG NG NH LH ?

LF	NG	MH	NF	MF
a	b	c	d	e

44

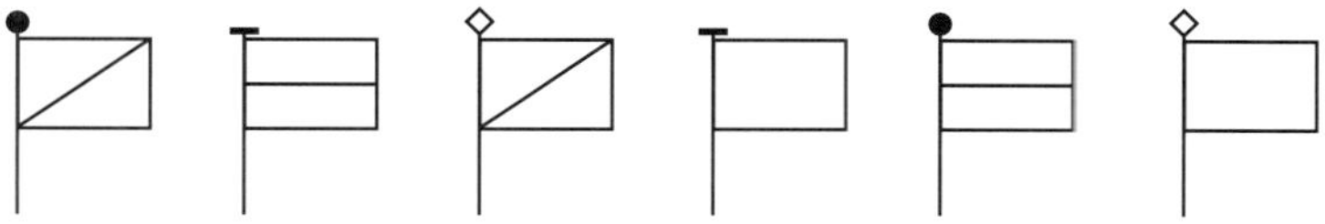

DL FS PL FB DS ?

PL	FL	DB	PS	PB
a	b	c	d	e

45

HE BF NE HF NF ?

BF	HF	HE	BE	NE
a	b	c	d	e

46

OT SC OE RC SE ?

RE	RT	OT	ST	OC
a	b	c	d	e

47

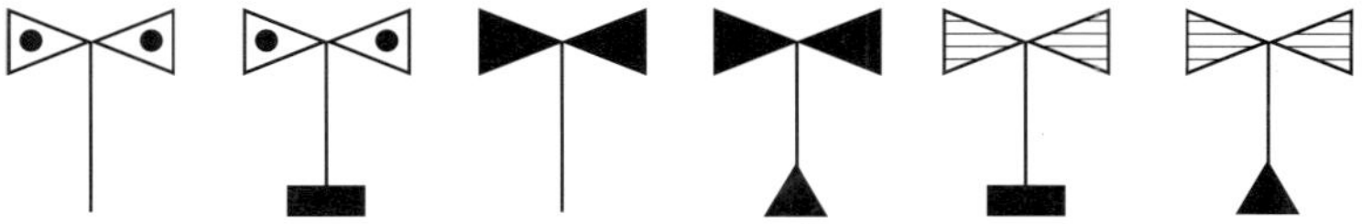

PS RS PU QU RT ?

PT	QU	QT	PS	RT
a	b	c	d	e

48

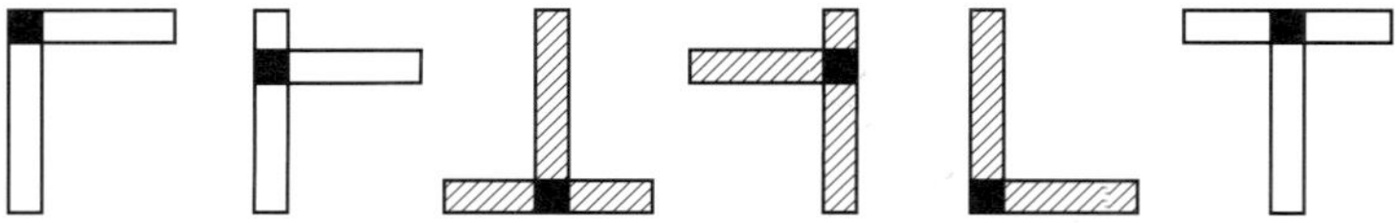

CX JX TY JY CY ?

JX	TX	TY	CY	JX
a	b	c	d	e

Find the shape or pattern which completes the square. Circle the letter.

Example

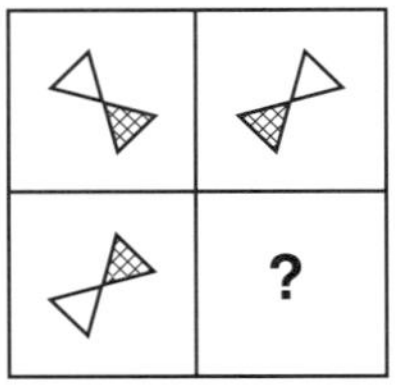

a b c d e

49

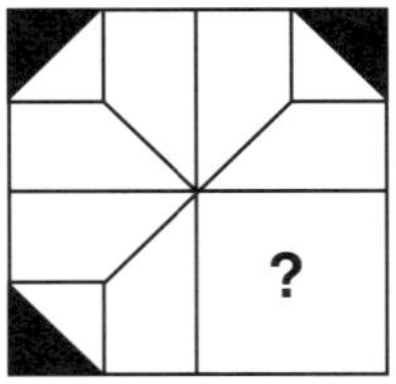

a b c d e

50

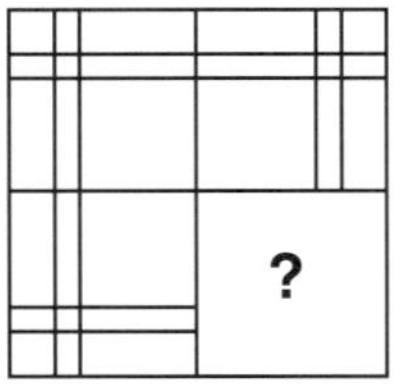

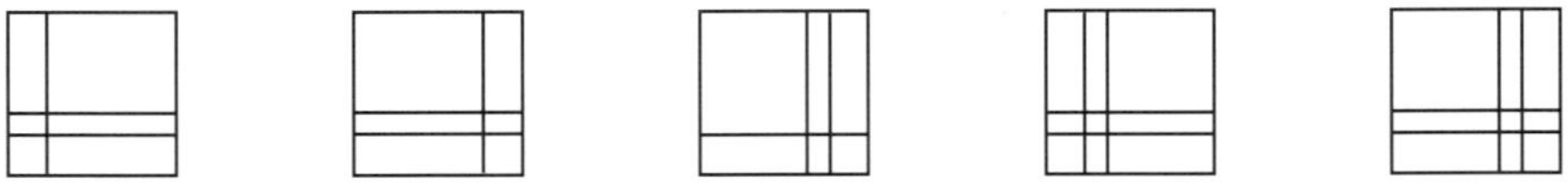

a b c d e

51

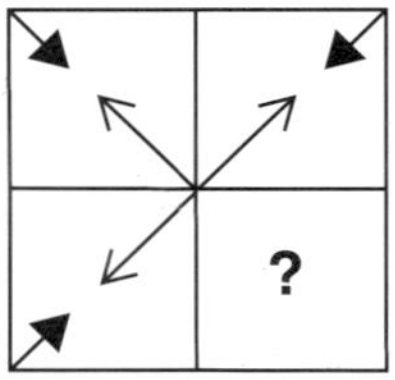

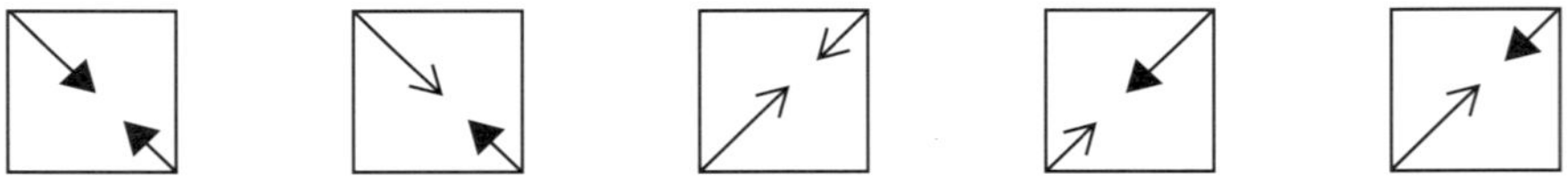

a b c d e

52

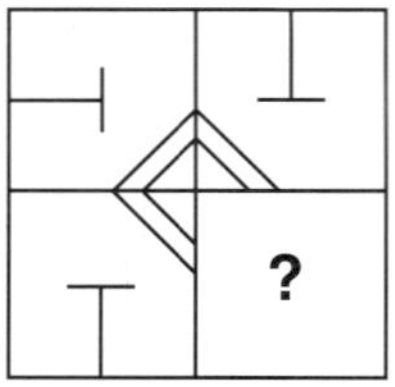

a b c d e

53

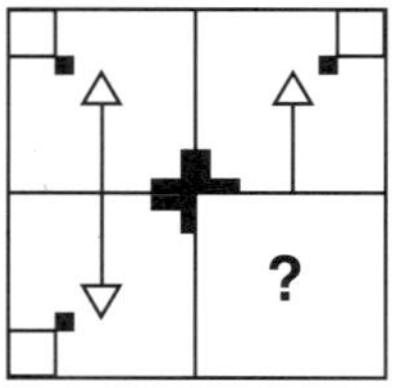

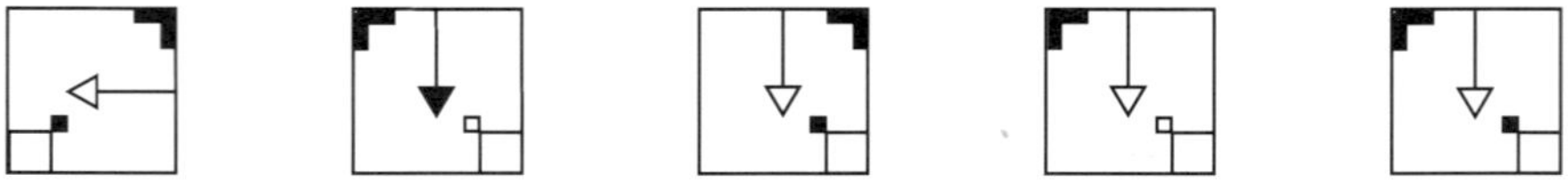

a b c d e

54

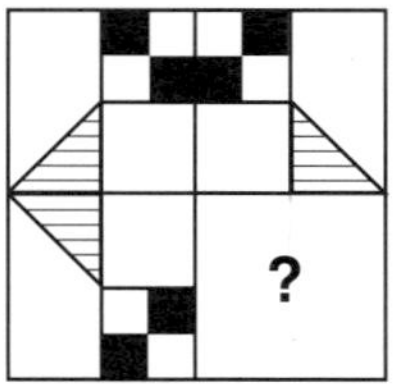

a b c d e

55

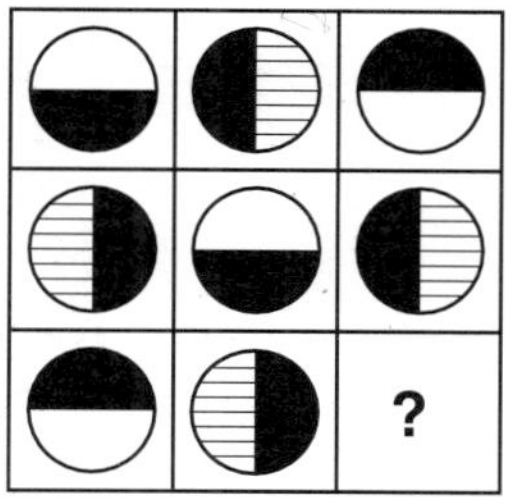

a b c d e

56

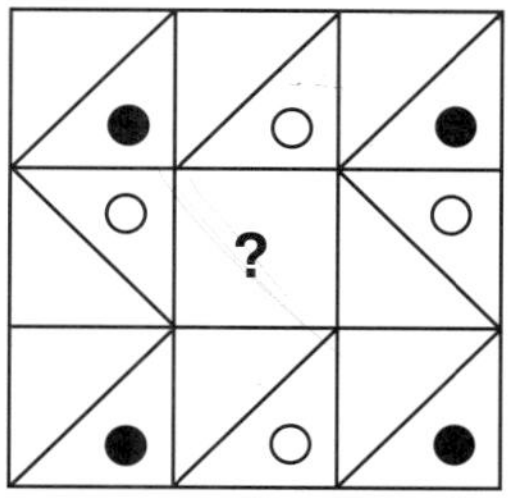

a b c d e

57

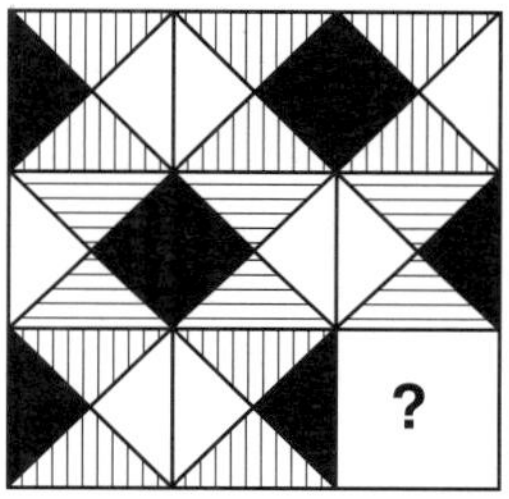

a b c d e

58

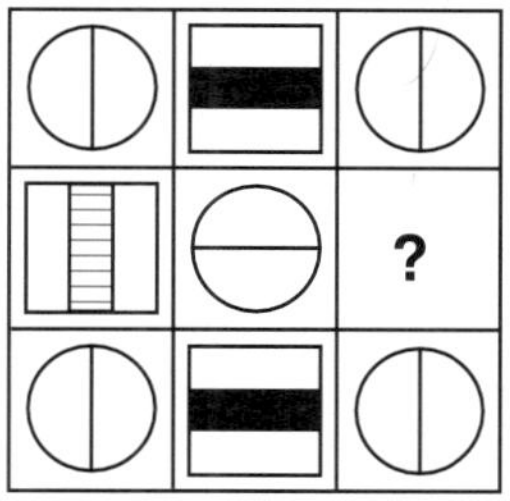

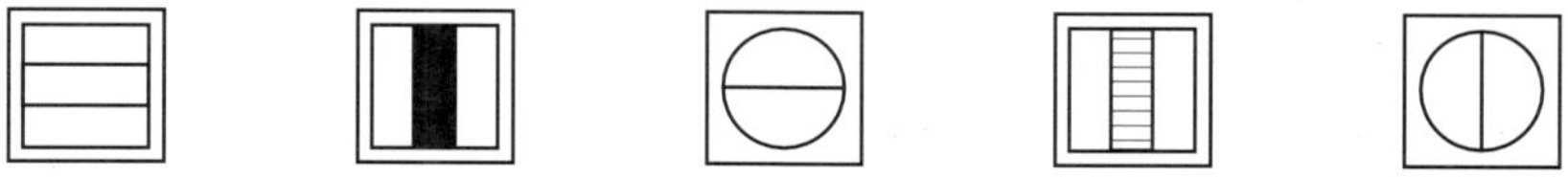

a b c d e

59

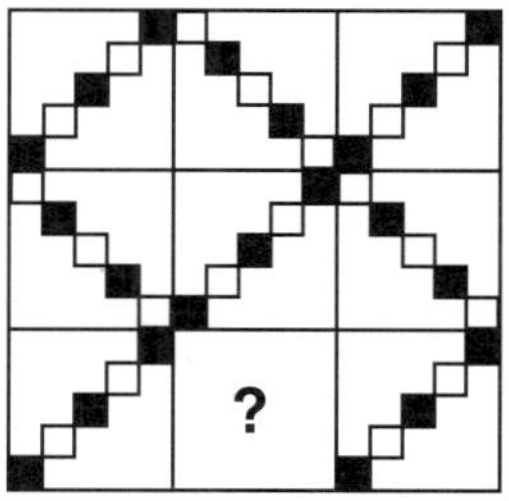

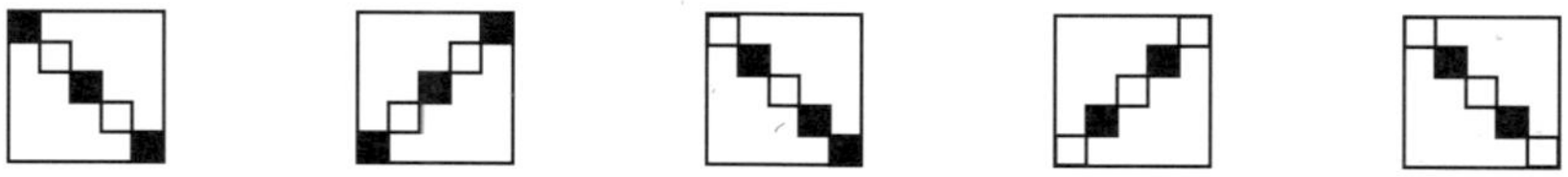

a b c d e

60

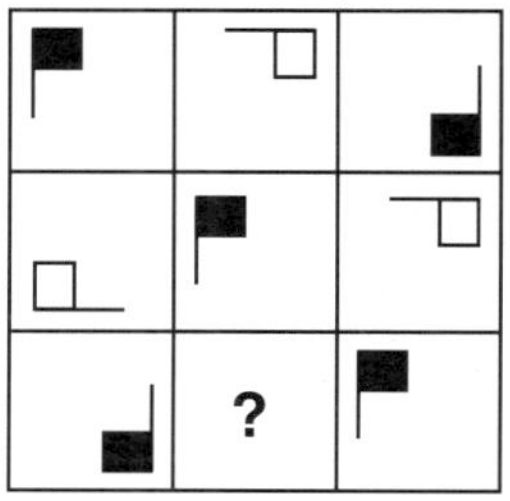

a b c d e

Paper 2

Find the shape or pattern which completes the second pair in the same way as the first pair. Circle the letter.

Example

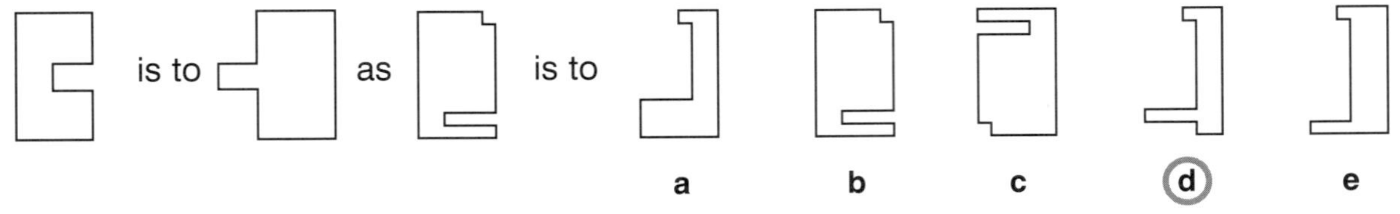

1

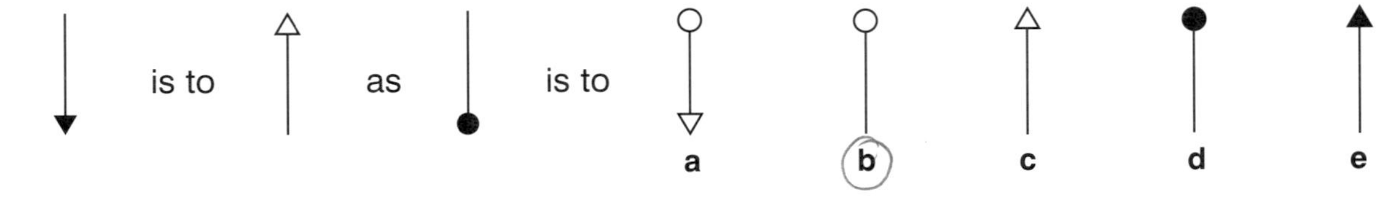

2

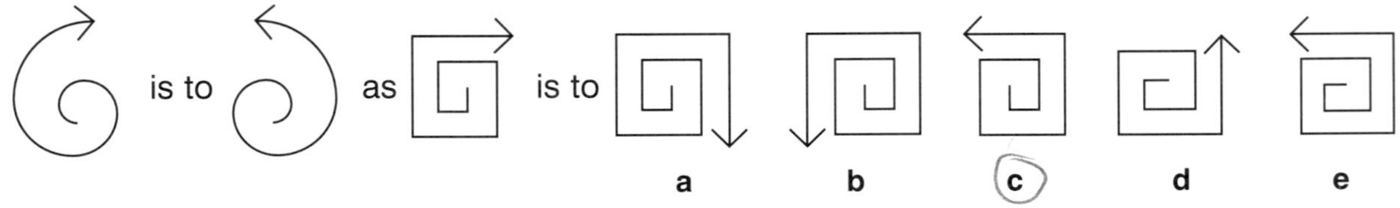

3

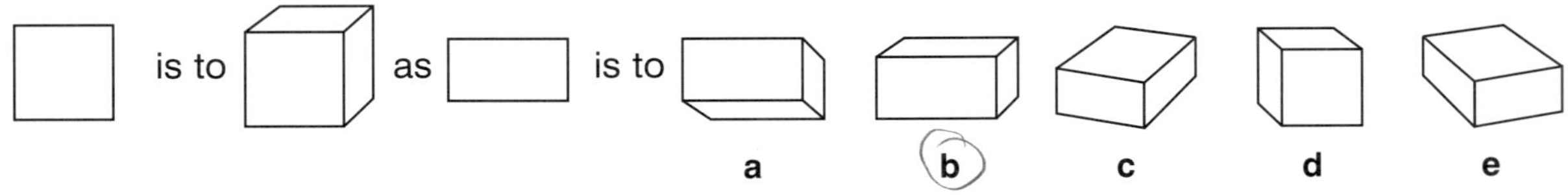

4

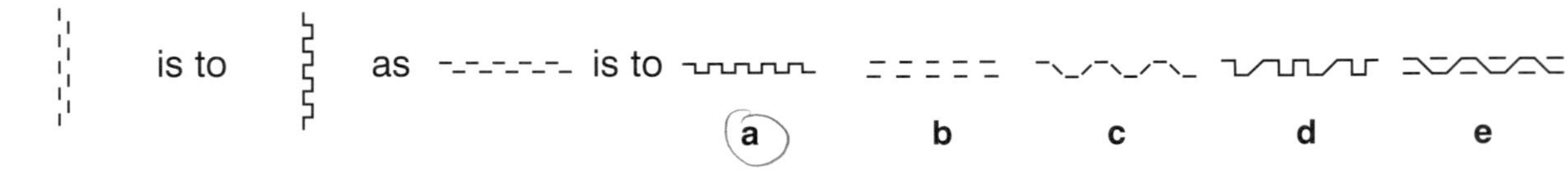

5

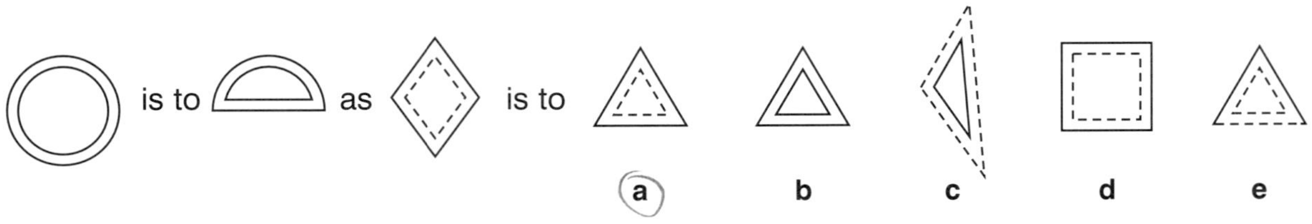

6

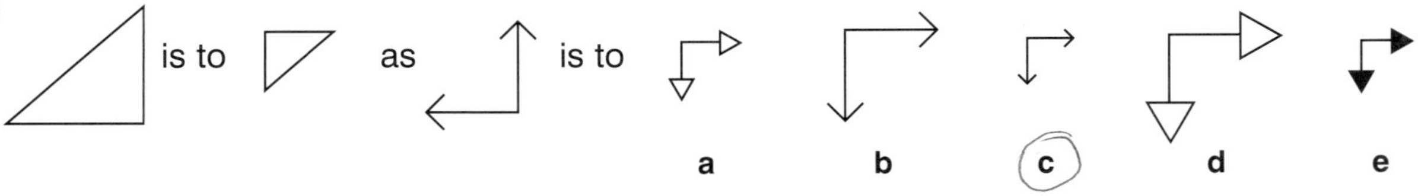

7

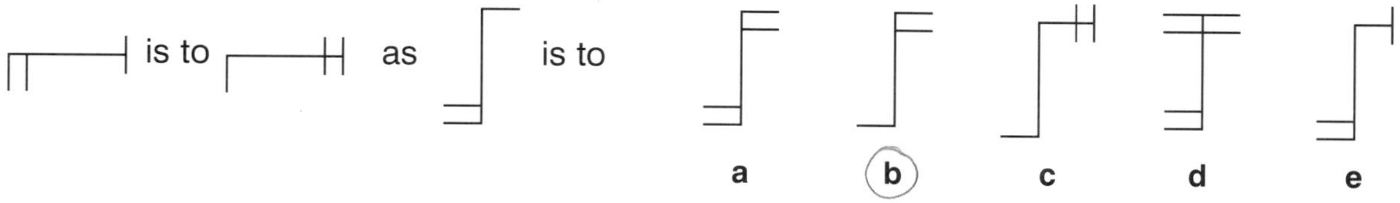
is to
as
is to
a
b
c
d
e

8

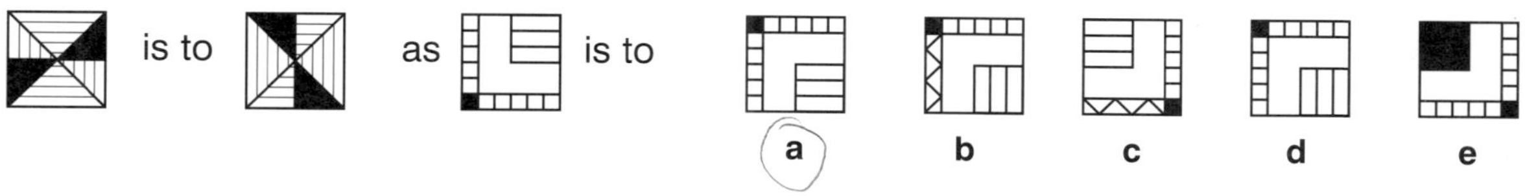
is to
as
is to
a
b
c
d
e

9

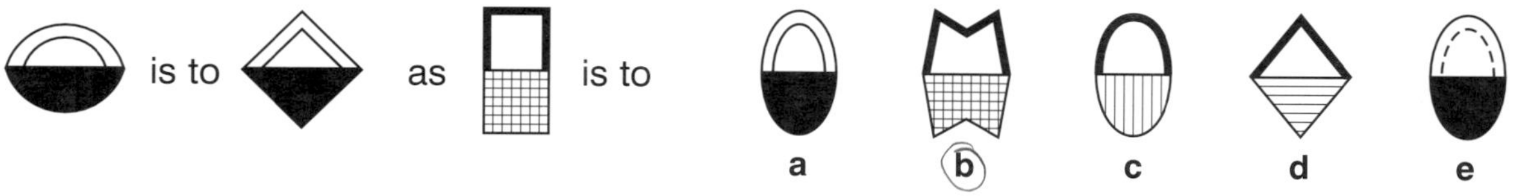
is to
as
is to
a
b
c
d
e

10

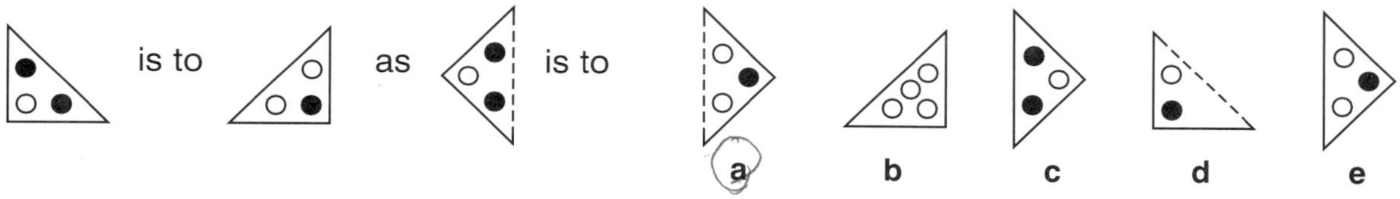
is to
as
is to
a
b
c
d
e

11

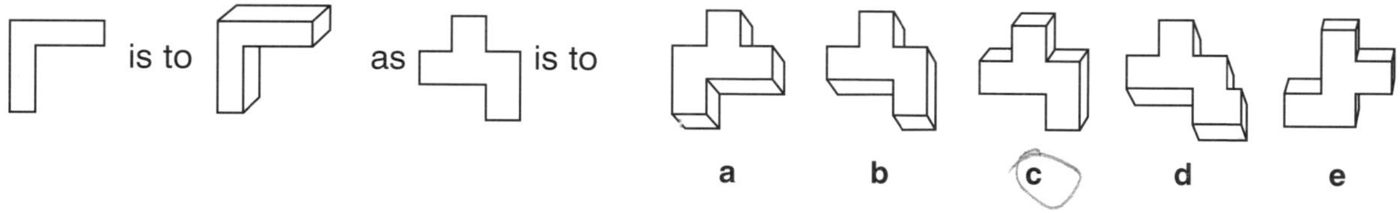
is to
as
is to
a
b
c
d
e

12

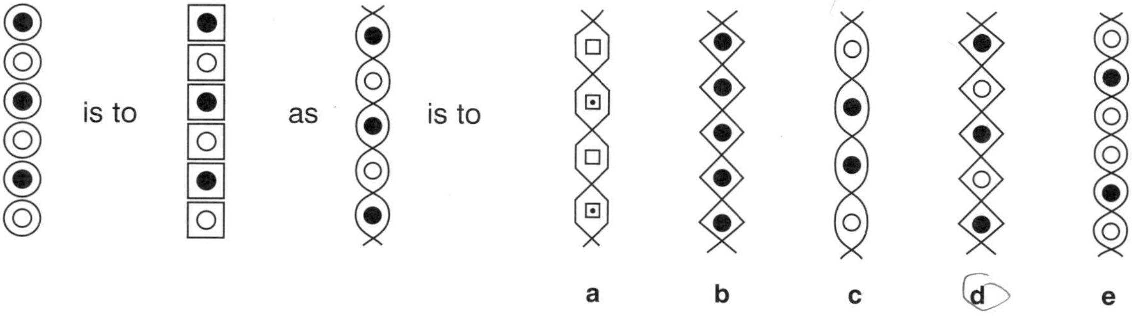
is to
as
is to
a
b
c
d
e

Find the shape or pattern which completes or continues the given series. Circle the letter.

Example

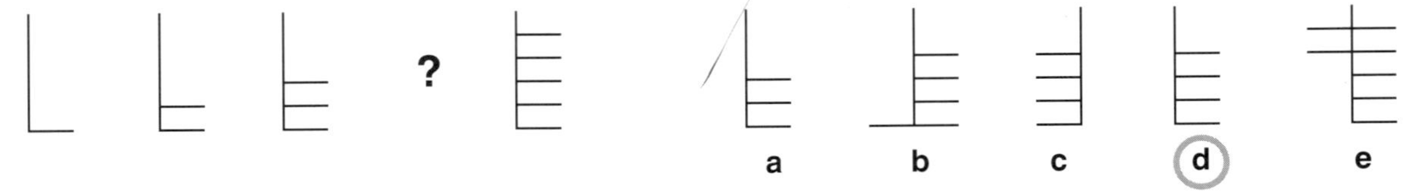

13

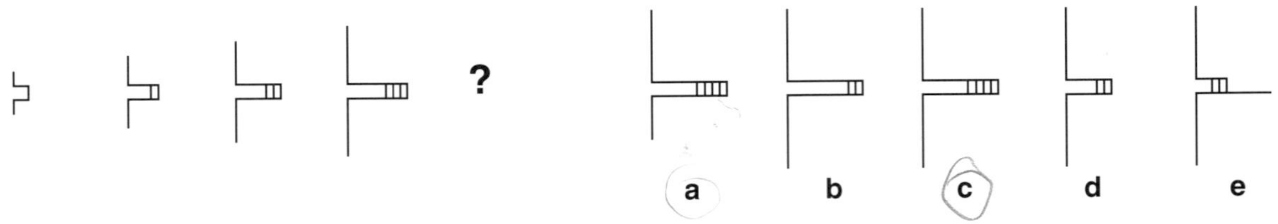

14

15

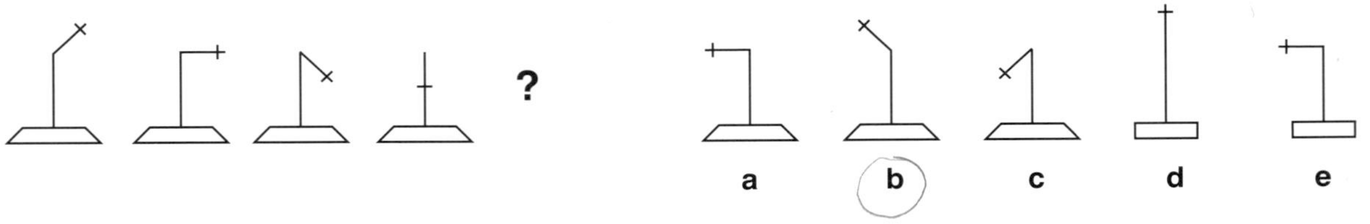

16

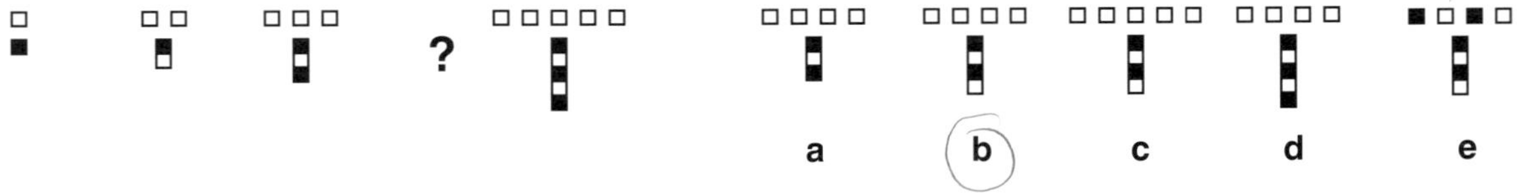

17

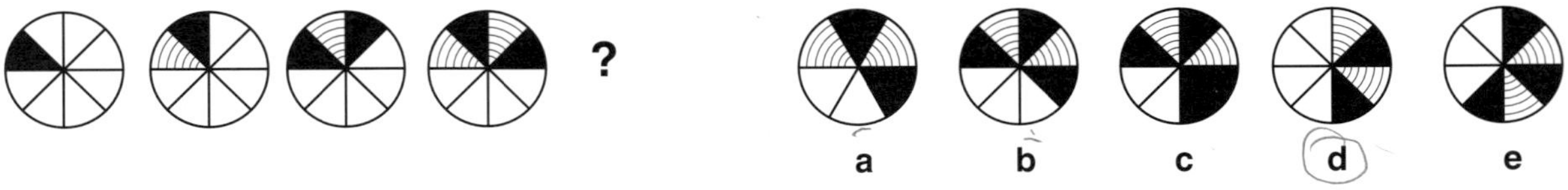

18

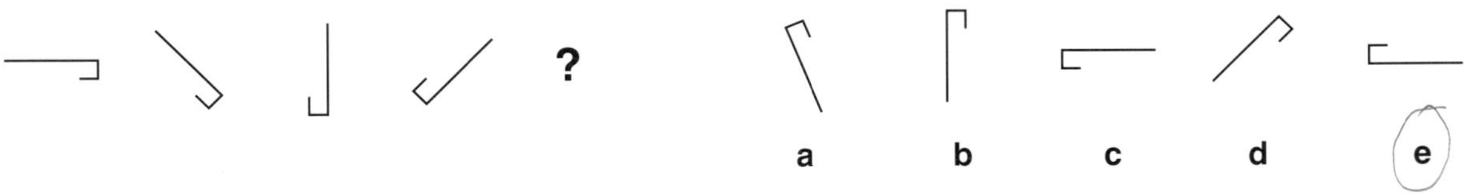

19

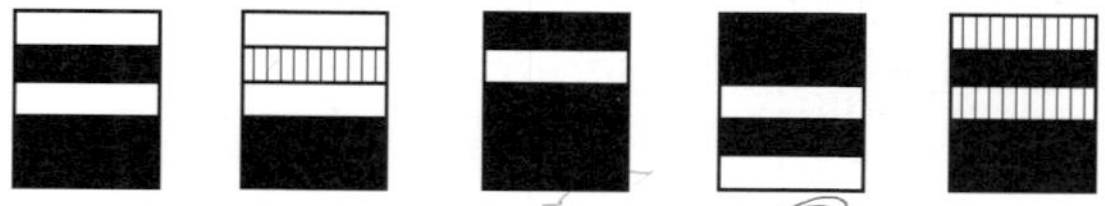

a b c d e

20

a b c d e

21

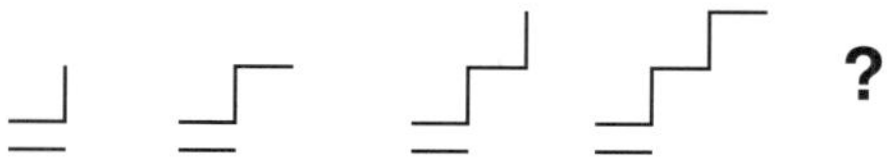

a b c d e

22

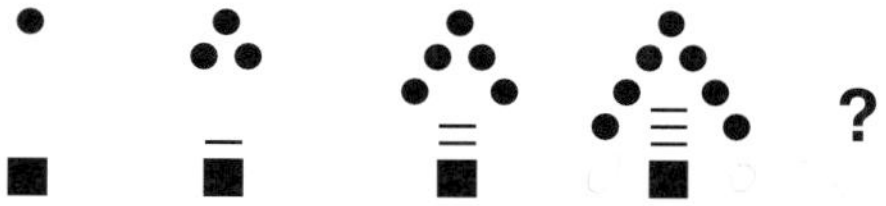

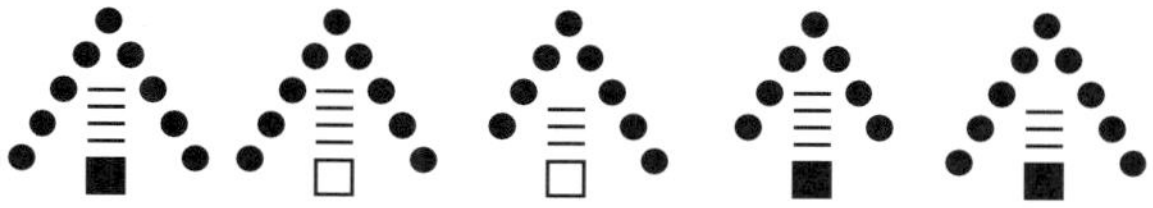

a b c d e

23

a b c d e

24

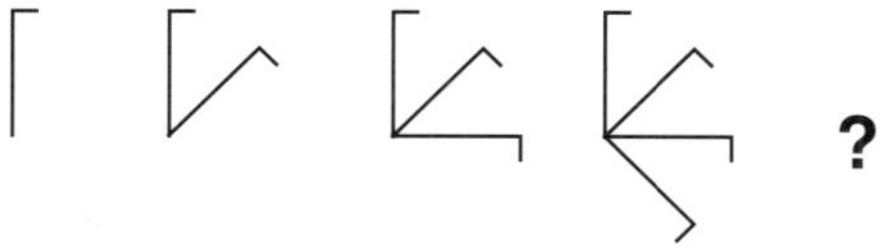

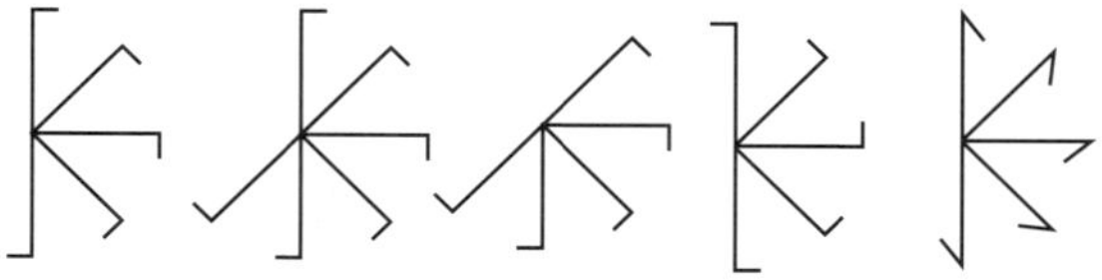

a b c d e

Look carefully at the shapes and codes given.
Select the code which matches the shape given at the end of each line.

Example

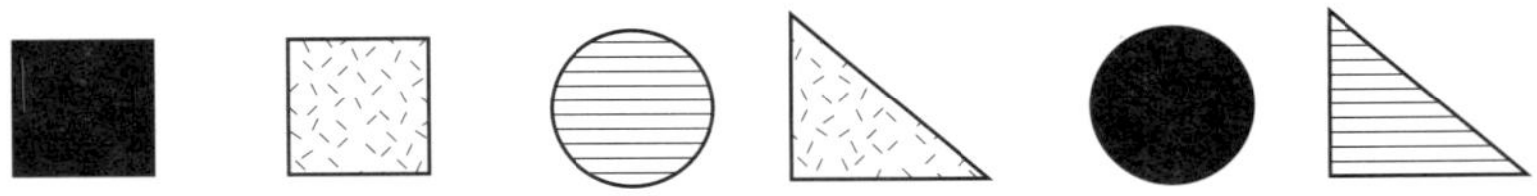

AX AY BZ CY BX ?

AY	AX	CZ	BZ	BY
a	b	c	d	e

25

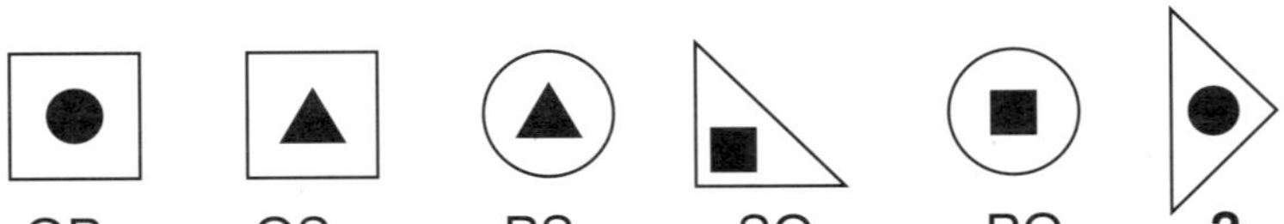

QR QS RS SQ RQ ?

SQ	SR	QR	QS	RS
a	b	c	d	e

26

XH YJ XP ZH ZJ ?

XH	YJ	ZH	XP	YP
a	b	c	d	e

27

PD FB PW AB AD ?

AW	PB	PD	FD	AB
a	b	c	d	e

28

KF LE MG MF KE ?

KG	LF	ME	LG	KF
a	b	c	d	e

29

NX MY NY QX MZ ?

MZ	QZ	QY	MX	NZ
a	b	c	d	e

30

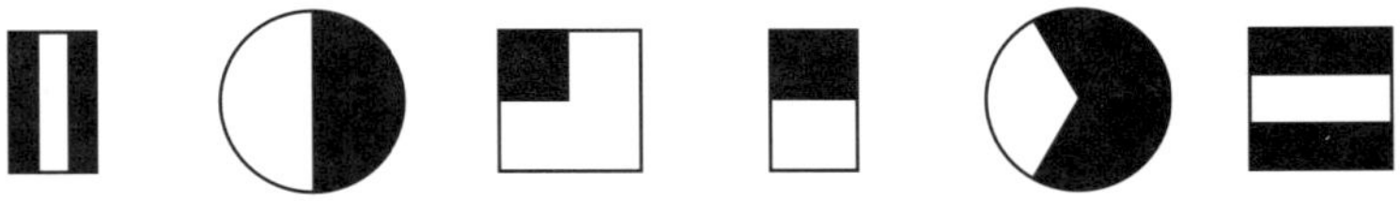

TR EP DS ER TP ?

DR	TS	DP	ES	TR
a	b	c	d	e

Which shape is most similar to the shapes in the group on the left? Circle the letter.

Example

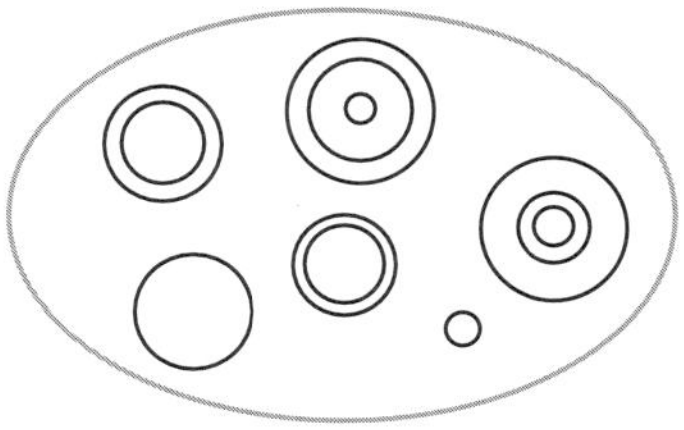

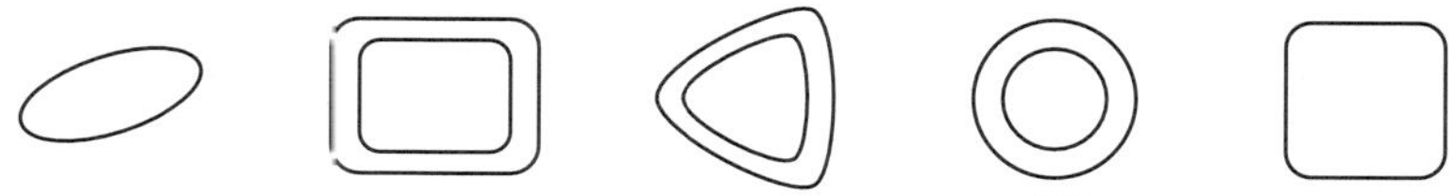

a b c d e

31

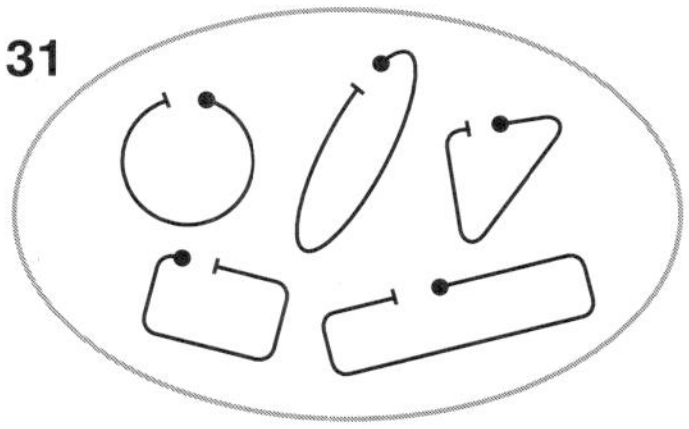

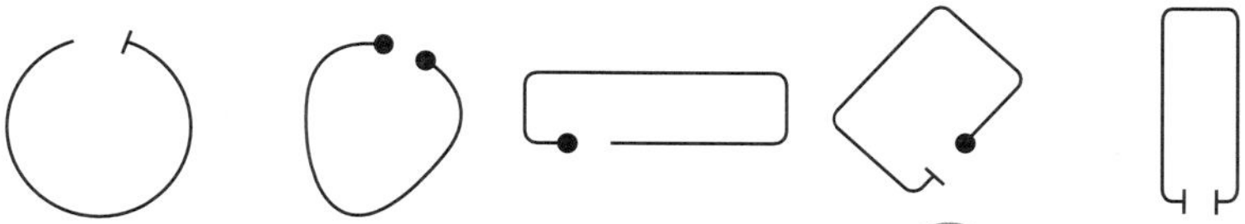

a b c d e

32

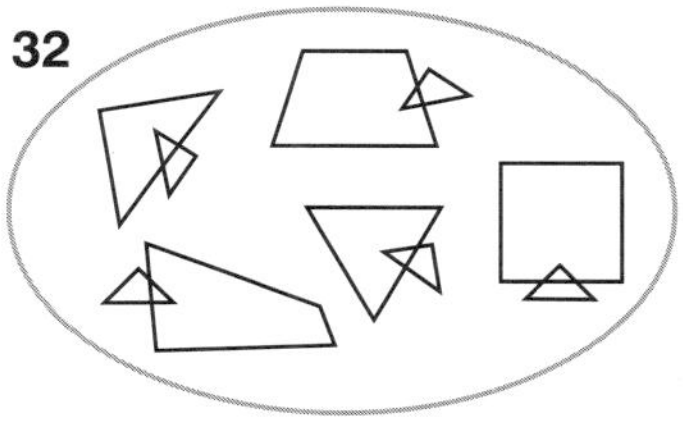

a b c d e

33

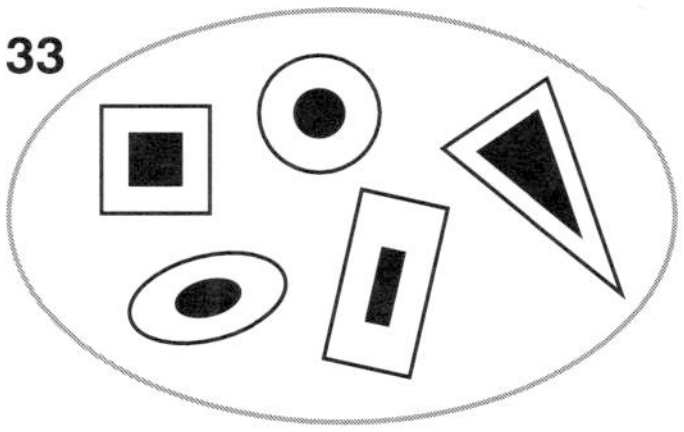

a b c d e

34

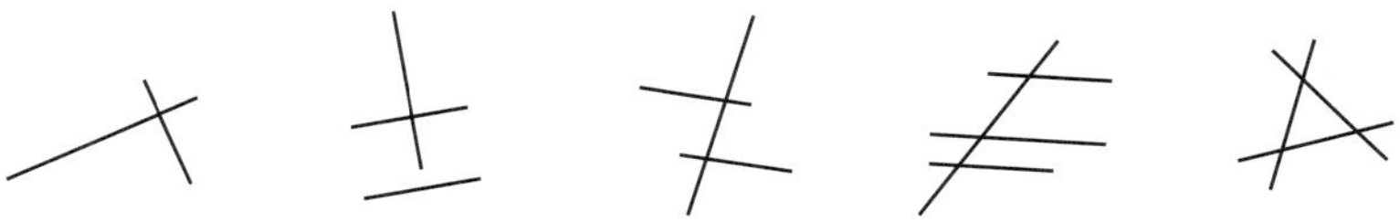

a b c d e

35

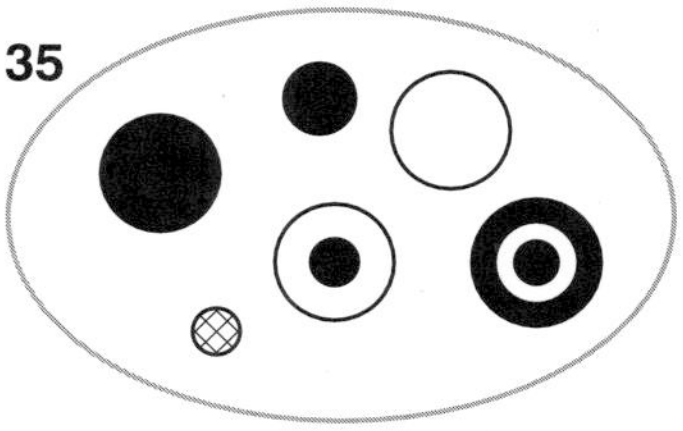

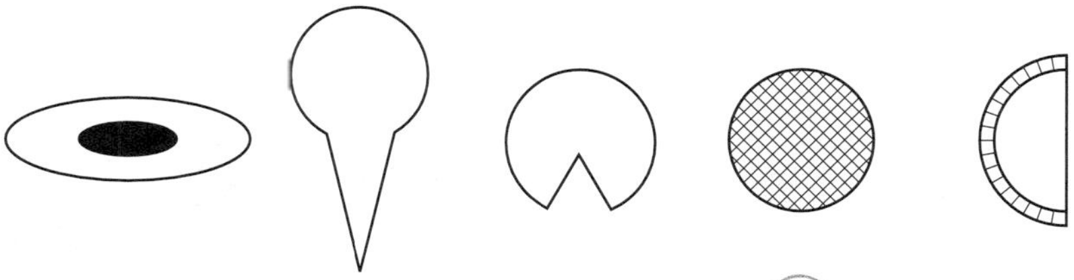

a b c d e

36

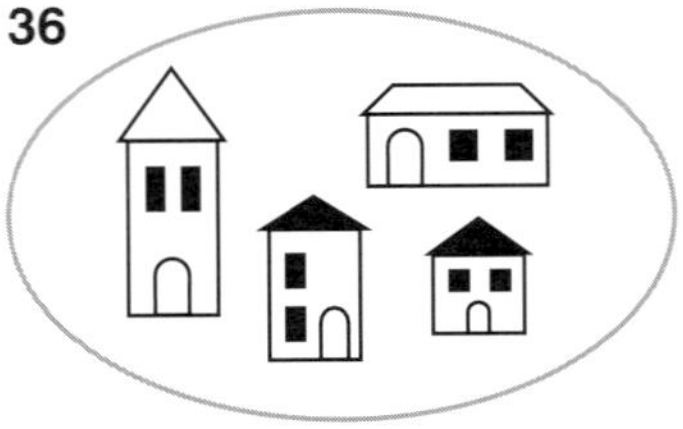

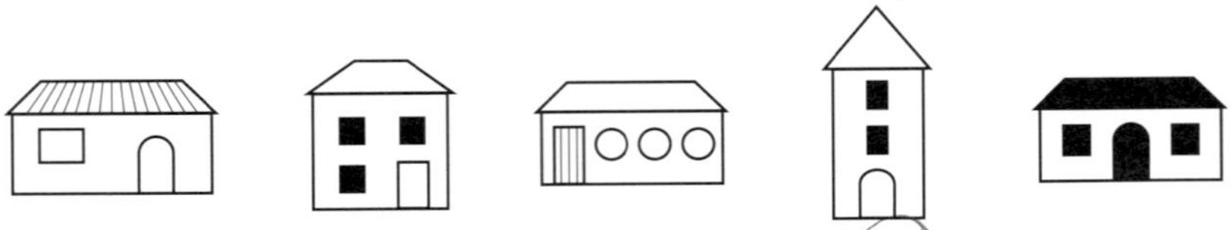

a **b** **c** **d** **e**

37

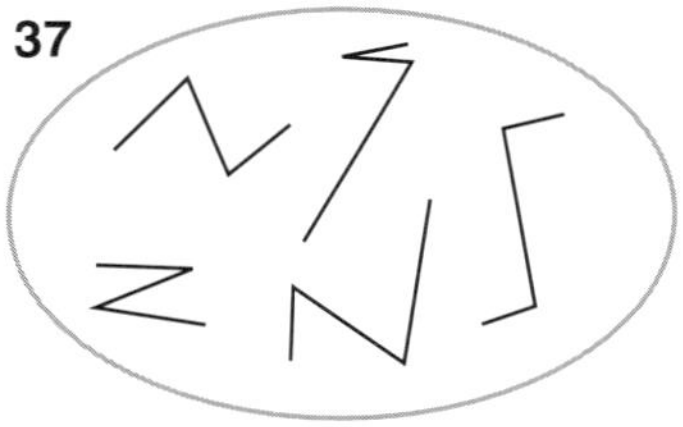

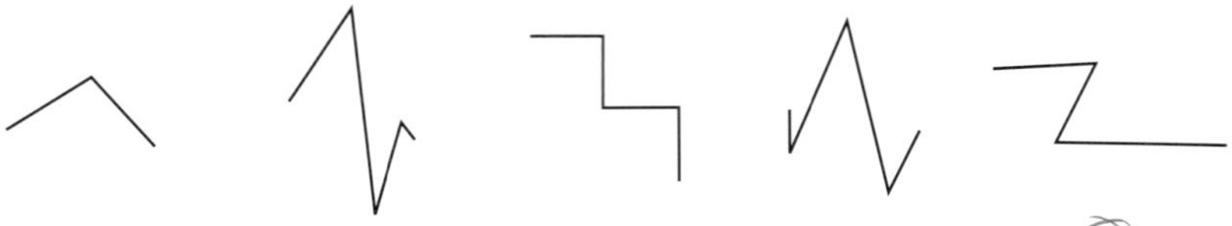

a **b** **c** **d** **e**

38

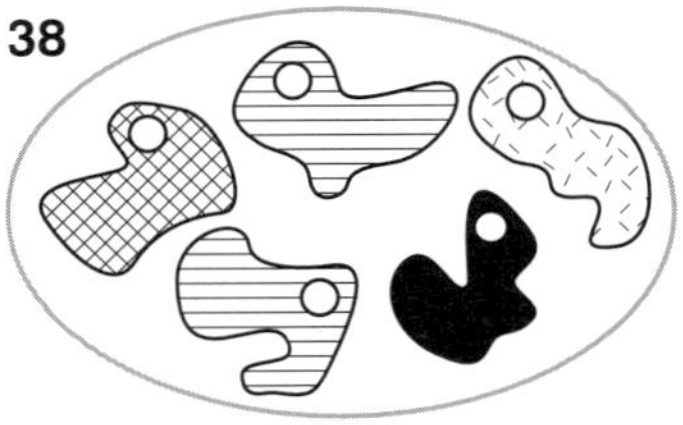

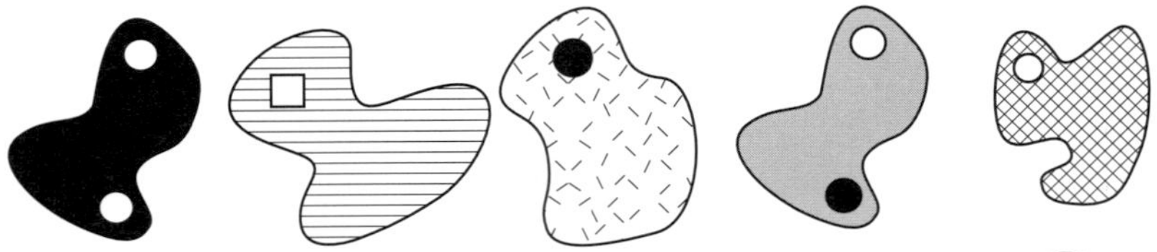

a **b** **c** **d** **e**

39

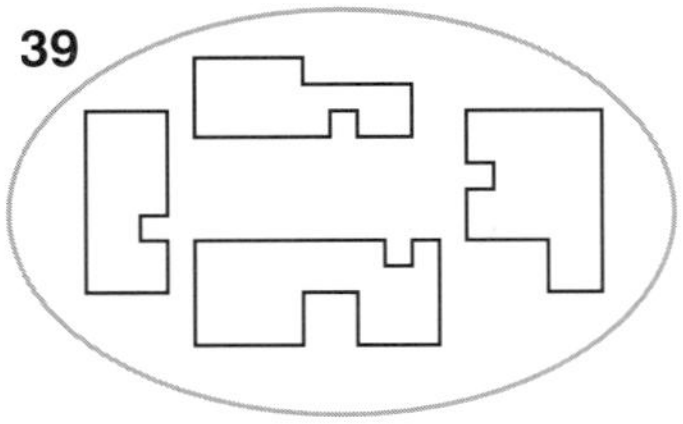

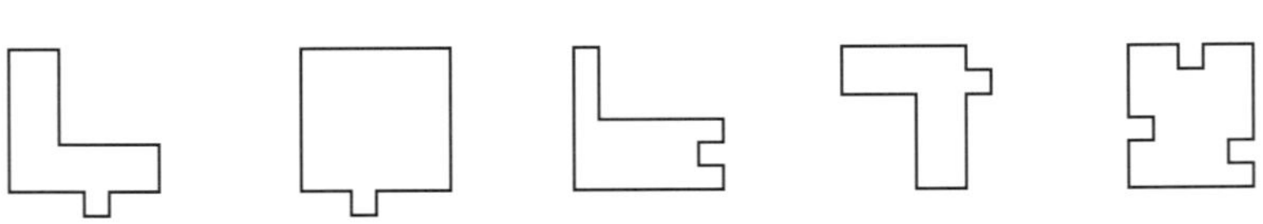

a **b** **c** **d** **e**

40

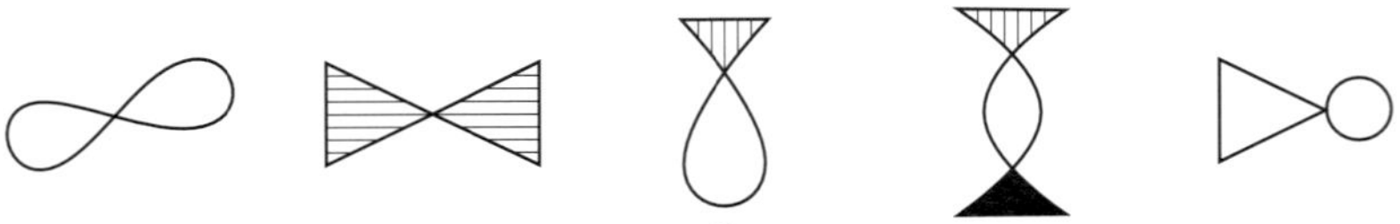

a **b** **c** **d** **e**

41

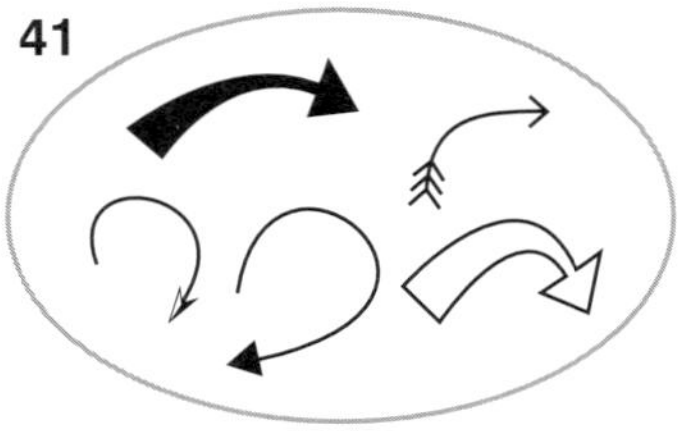

a **b** **c** **d** **e**

42

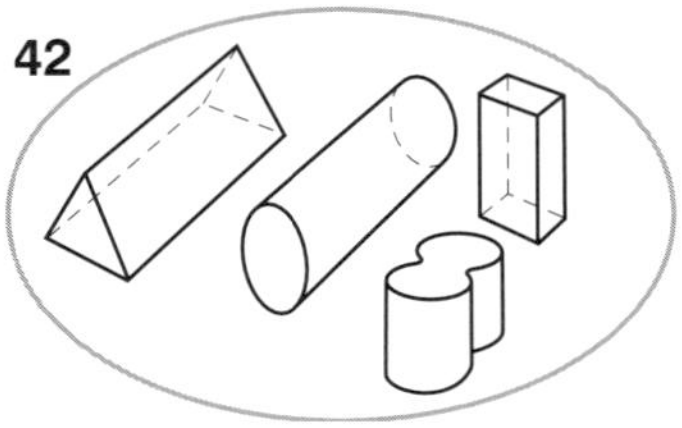

a **b** **c** **d** **e**

Find the shape or pattern which completes the square. Circle the letter.

Example

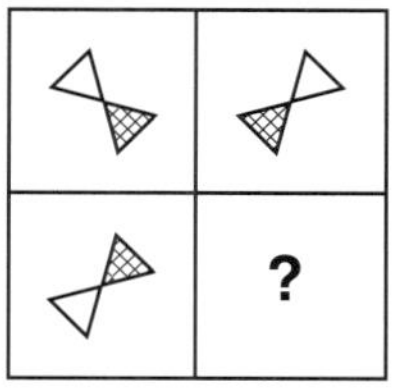

a b c d e

43

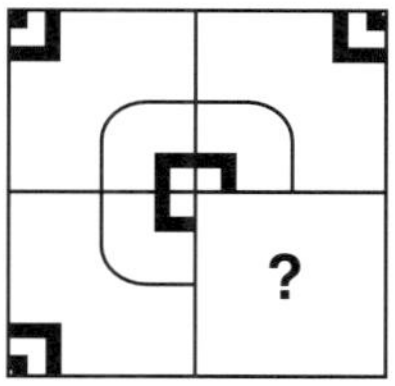

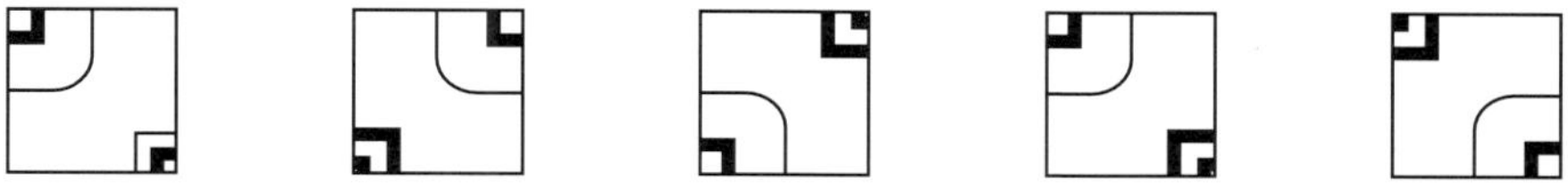

a b c d e

44

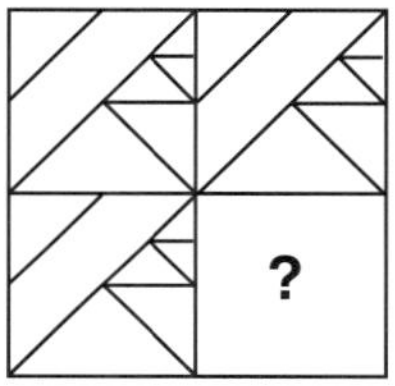

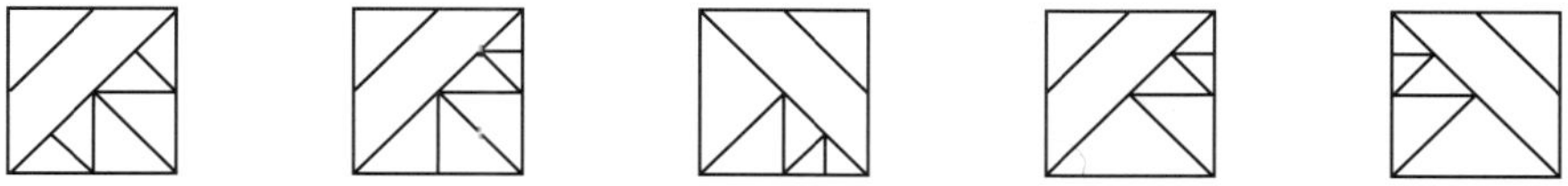

a b c d e

45

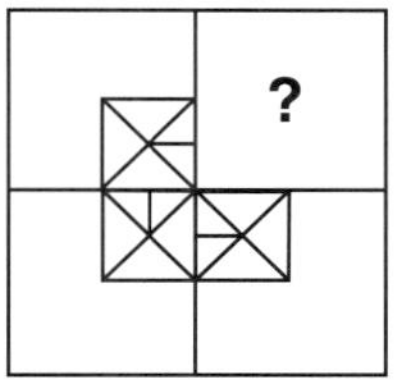

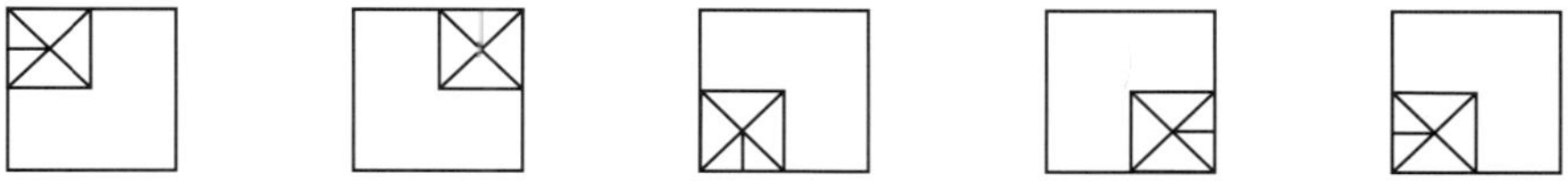

a b c d e

46

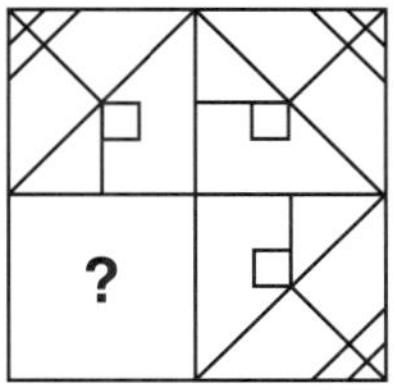

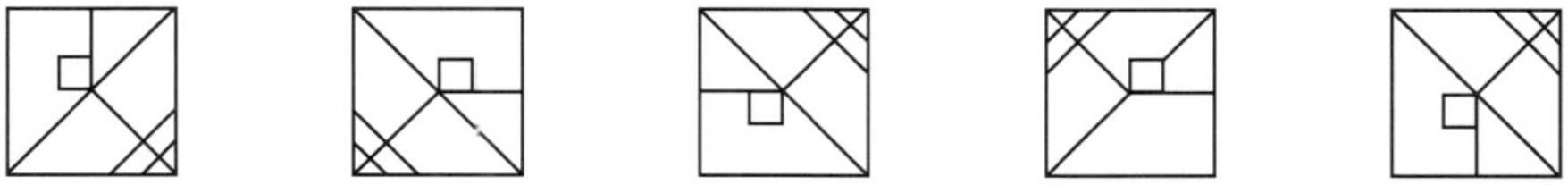

a b c d e

47

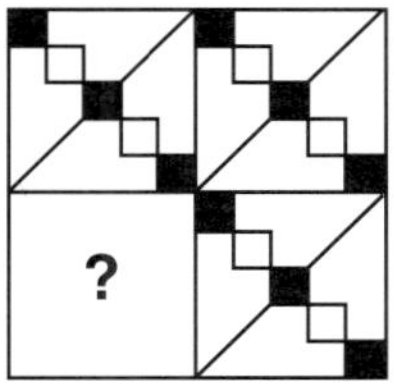

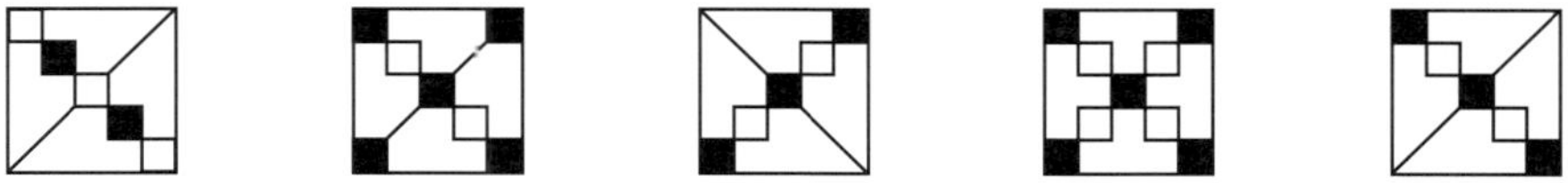

a b c d e

48

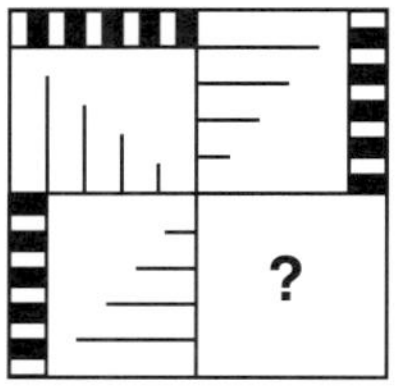

a b c d e

49

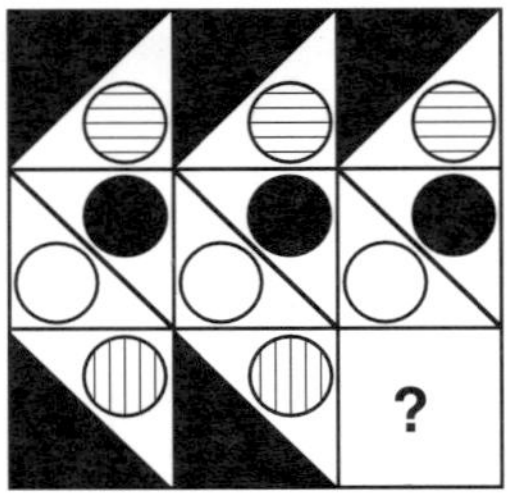

a b c d e

50

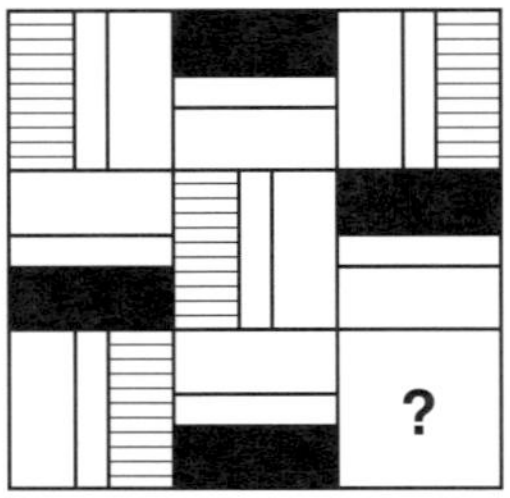

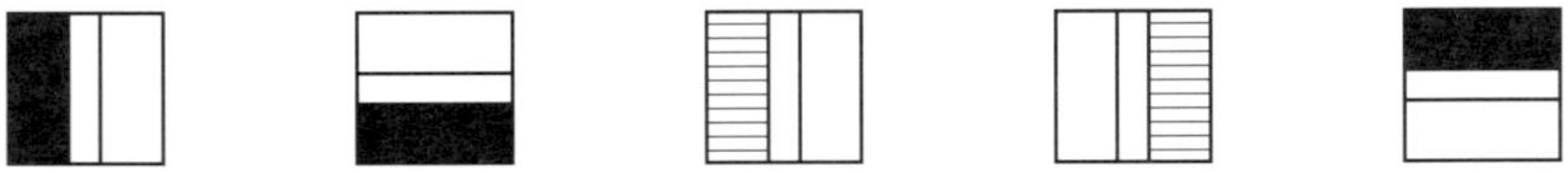

a b c d e

51

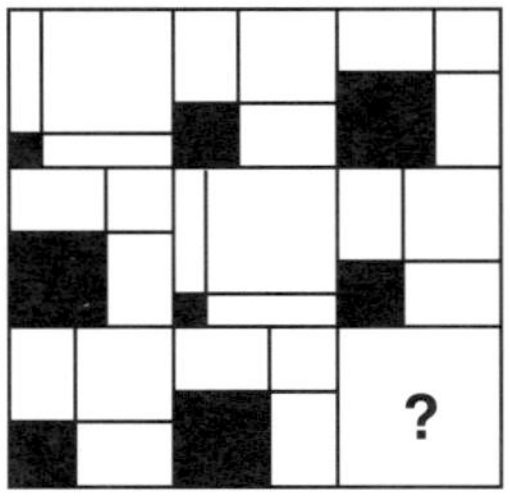

a b c d e

52

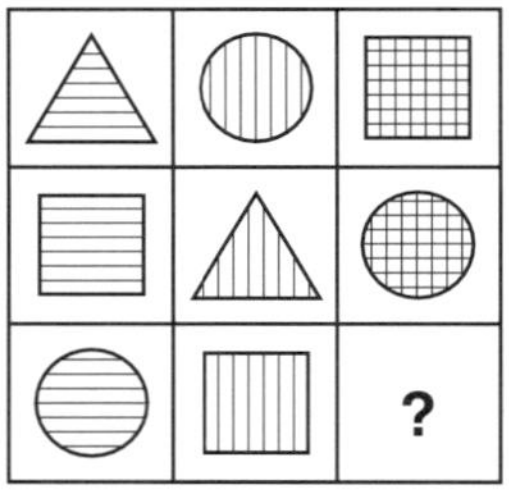

a b c d e

53

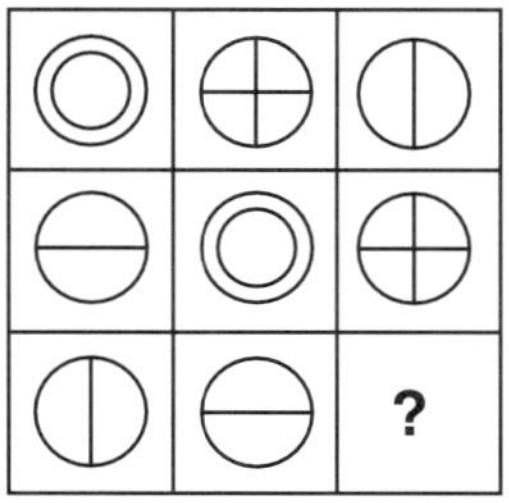

a b c d e

54

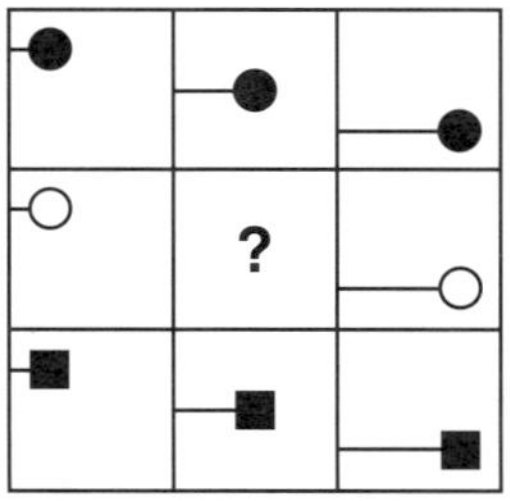

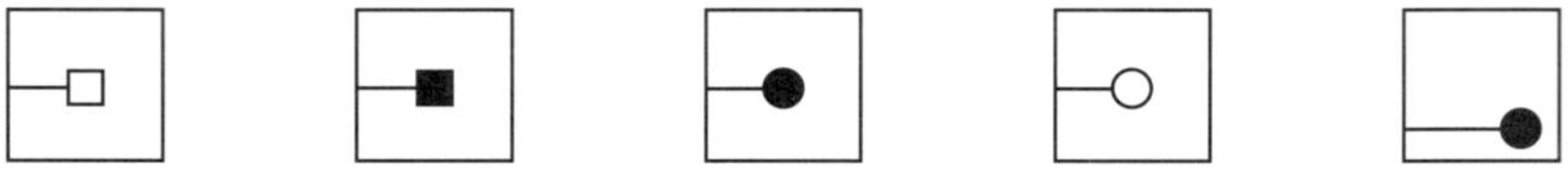

a b c d e

Which shape on the right is the reflection of the shape given on the left? Circle the letter.

Example

a b c d e

55

a b c d e

56

a b c d e

57

a b c d e

58

a b c d e

59

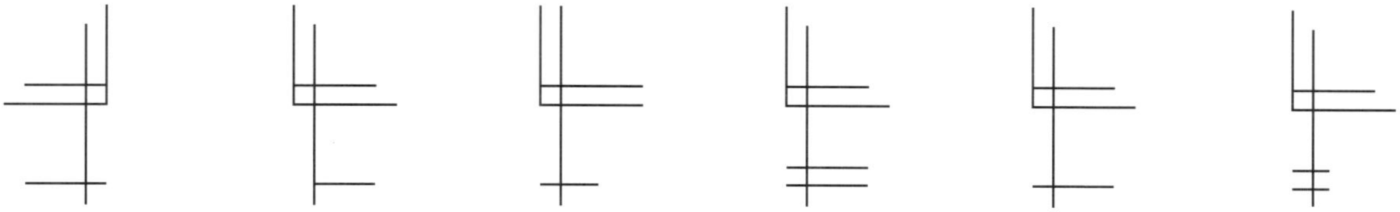

a b c d e

60

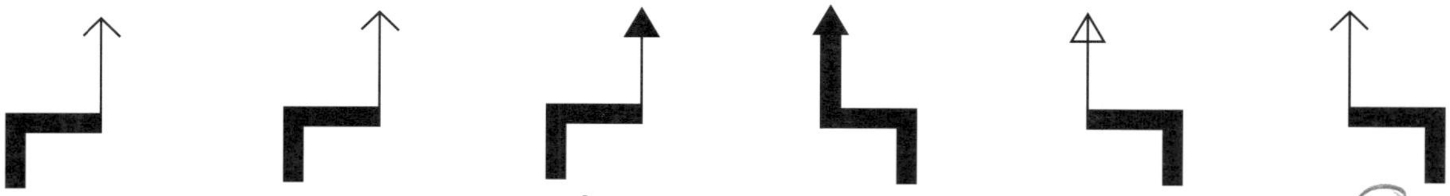

a b c d e

Paper 3

Which shape or pattern is most similar to the ones in the group on the left? Circle the letter.

Example

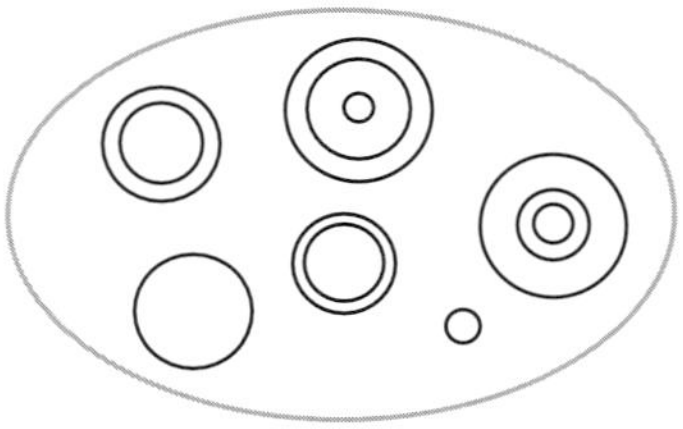

a b c d e

1

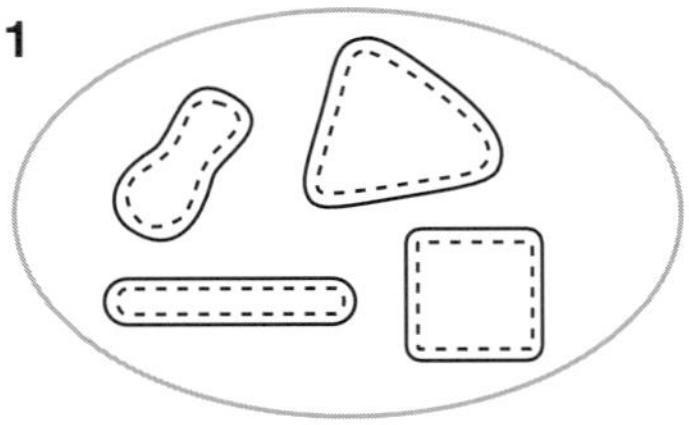

a b c d e

2

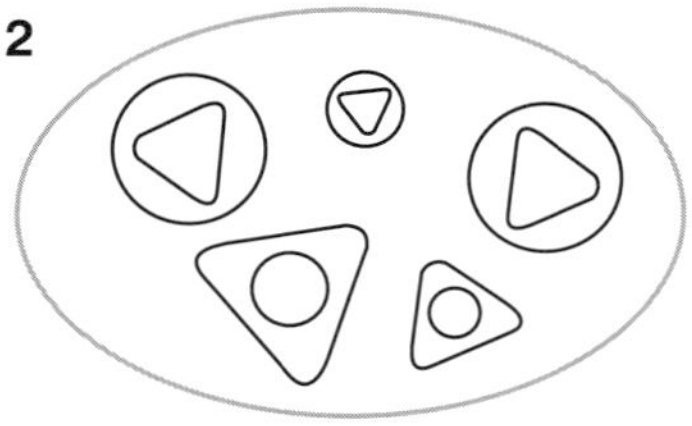

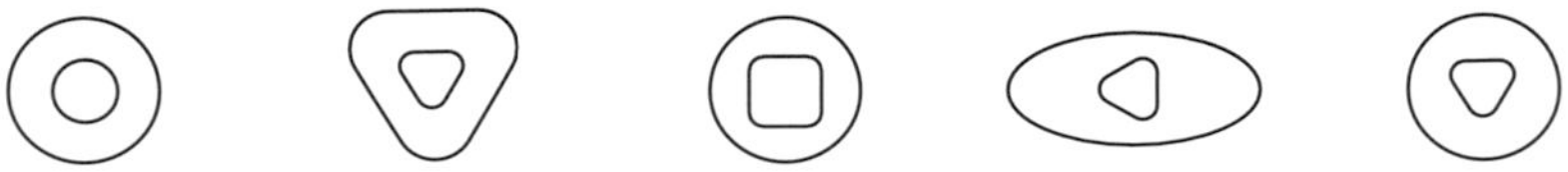

a b c d e

3

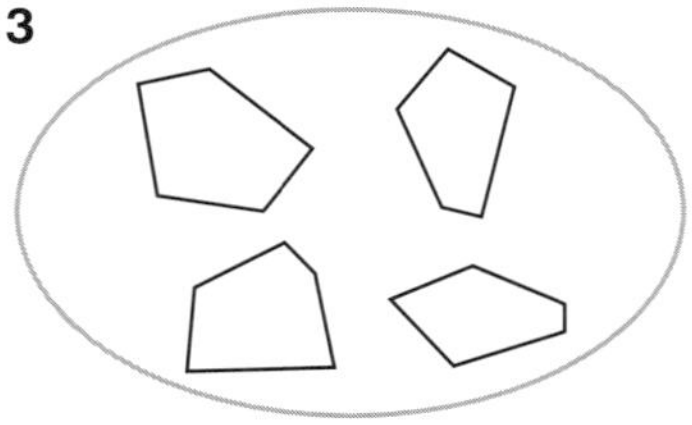

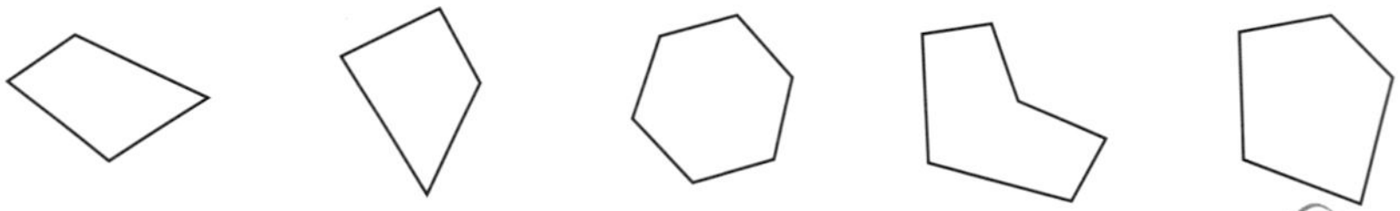

a b c d e

4

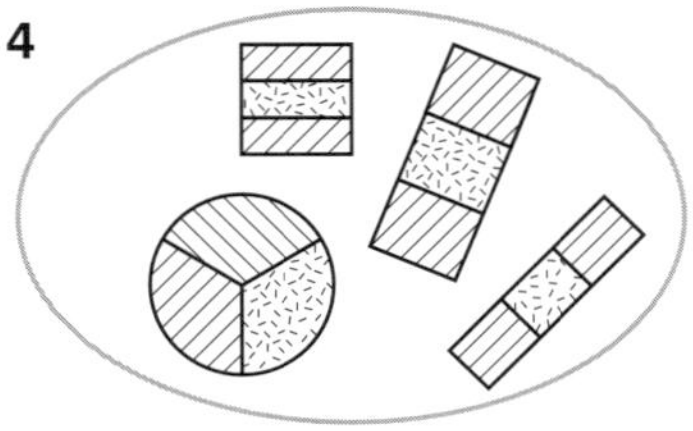

a b c d e

5

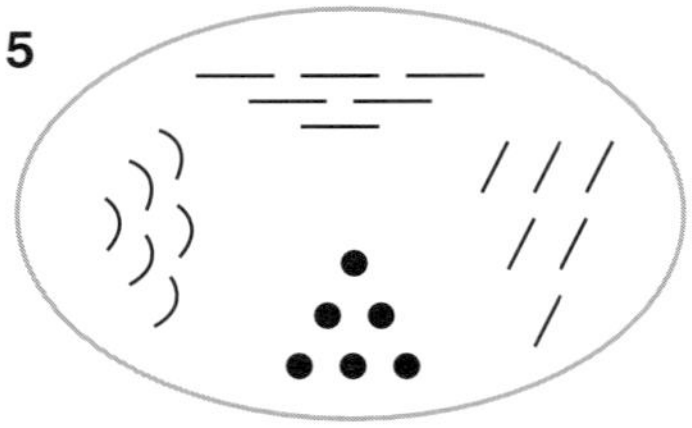

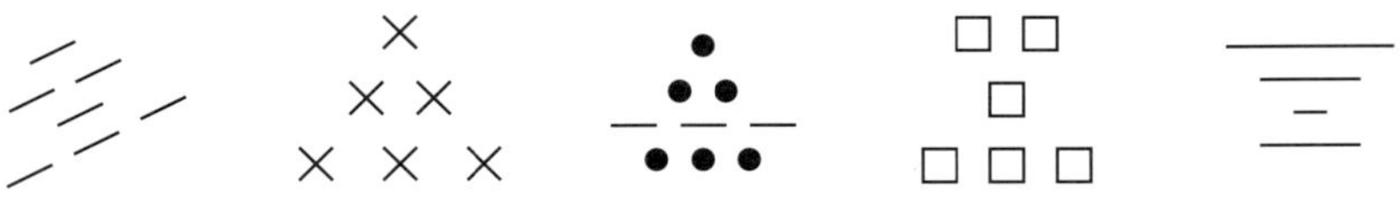

a b c d e

6

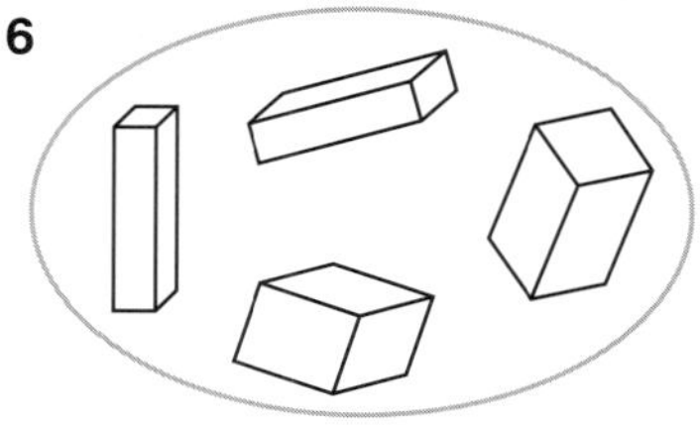

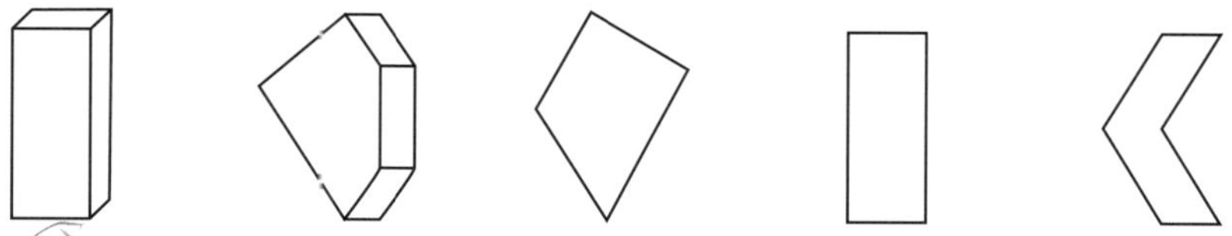

a b c d e

7

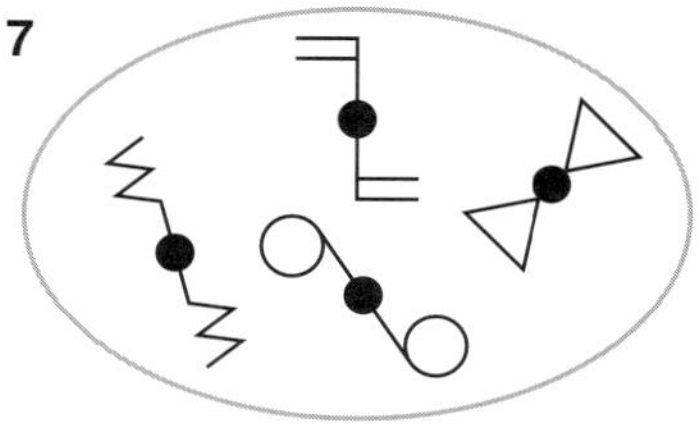

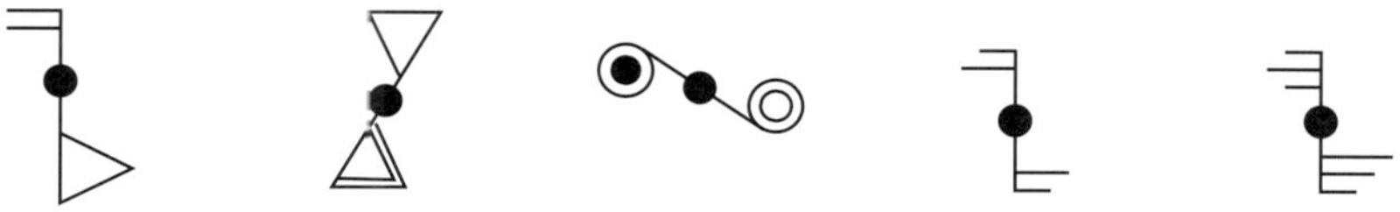

a b c d e

8

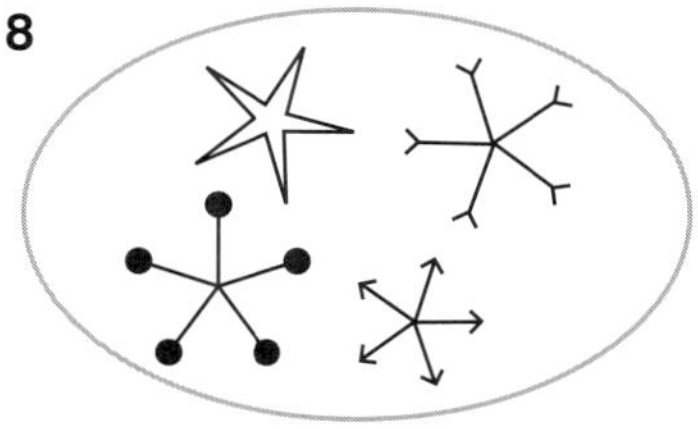

a b c d e

9

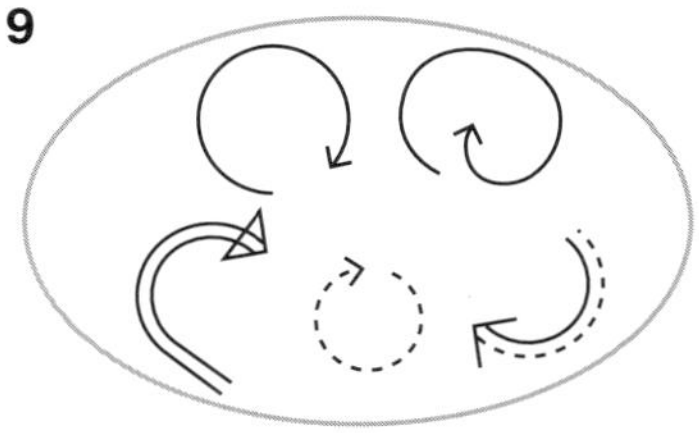

a b c d e

10

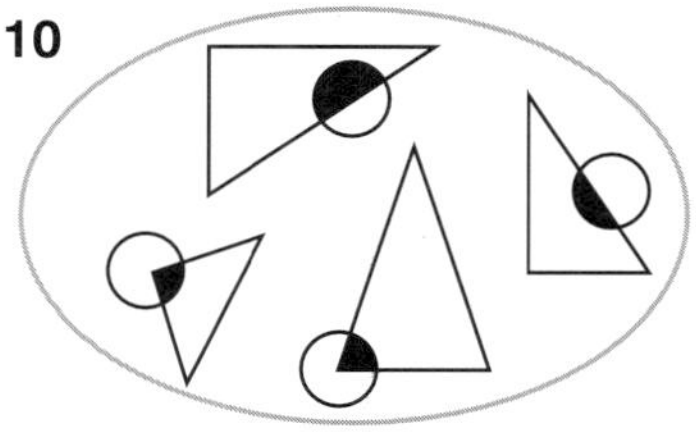

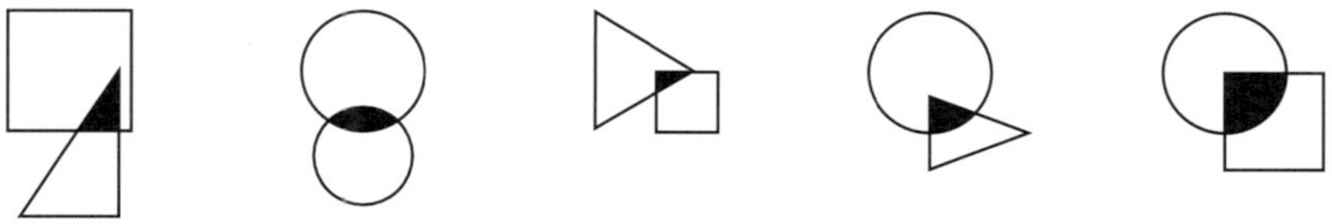

a b c d e

11

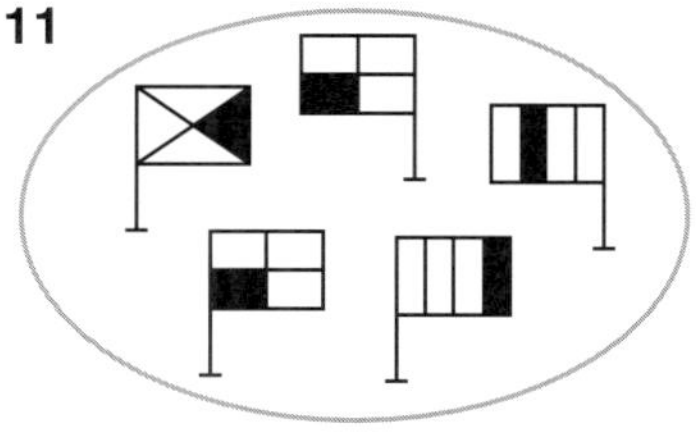

a b c d e

12

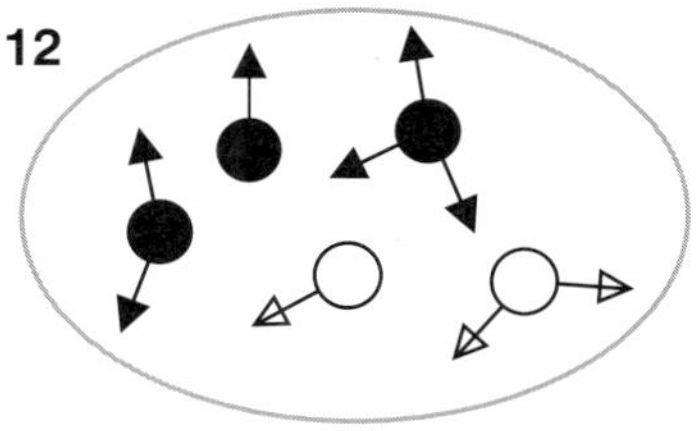

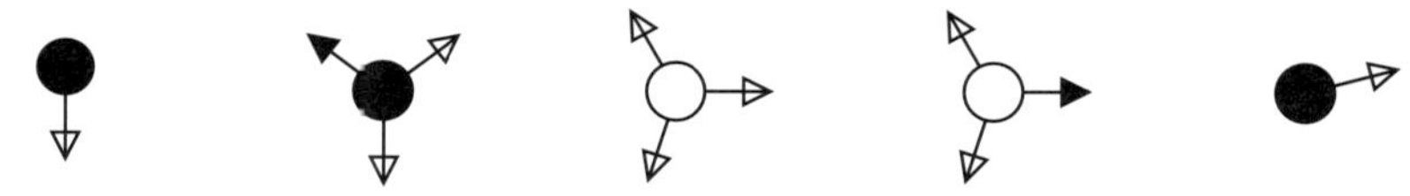

a b c d e

Find the shape or pattern which completes or continues the given series. Circle the letter.

Example

a b c d e

13

a b c d e

14

a b c d e

15

a b c d e

16

a b c d e

17

a b c d e

18

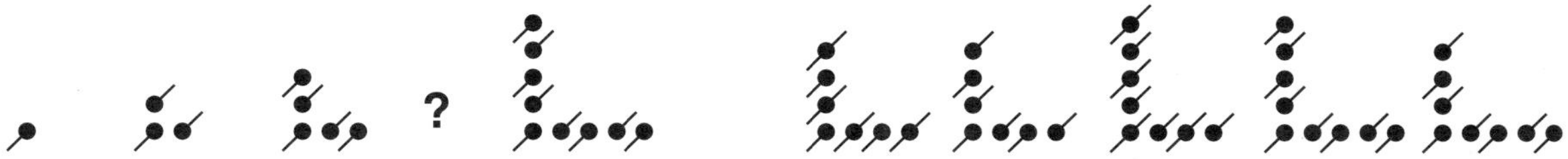

a b c d e

19

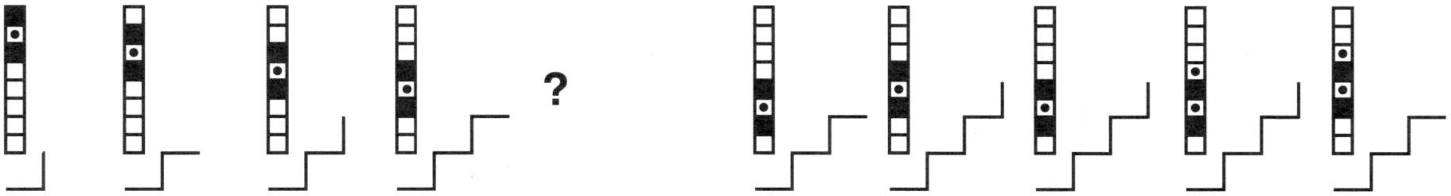

a b c d e

20

a b c d e

21

a b c d e

22

a b c d e

23

a b c d e

24

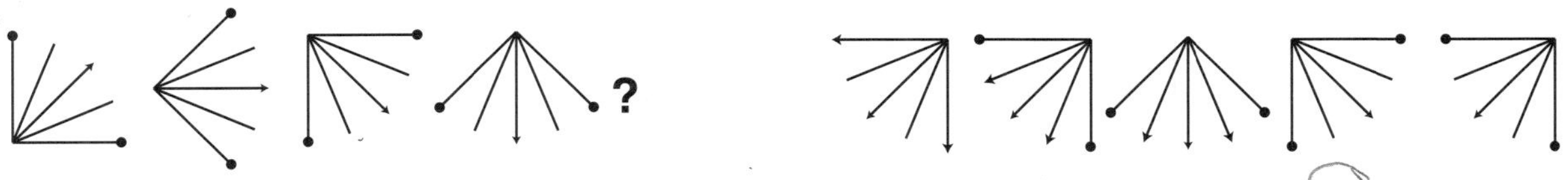

a b c d e

Look carefully at the shapes and codes given.
Select the code which matches the shape given at the end of each line.

Example

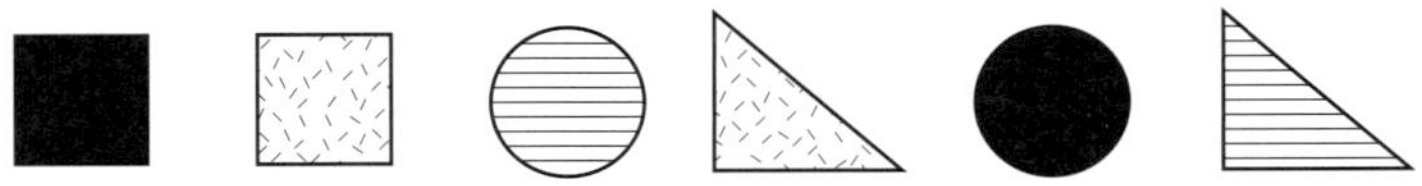

AX AY BZ CY BX ?

AY	AX	CZ	BZ	BY
a	b	c	d	e

25

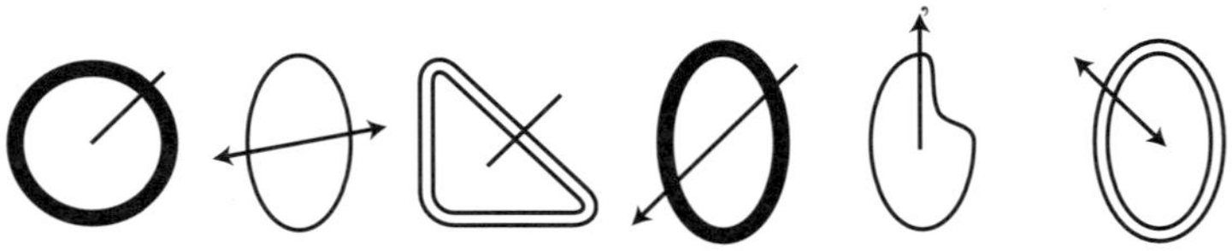

KX LY MX KZ LZ ?

KY	MX	LX	MY	KZ
a	b	c	d	e

26

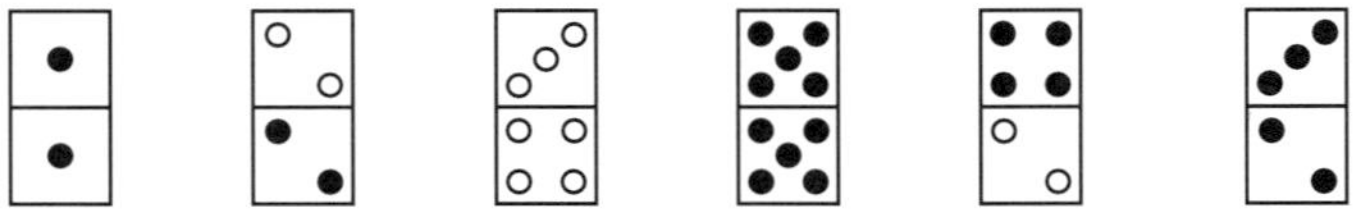

AT CT BS AT CS ?

BT	AT	AS	CS	BS
a	b	c	d	e

27

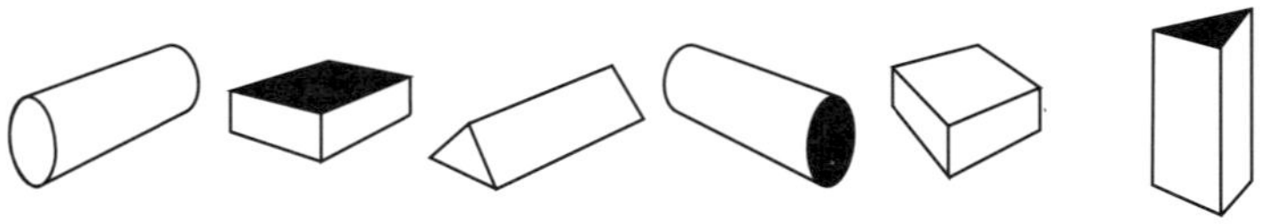

PC QO RC PO QC ?

RC	PO	QC	RO	PC
a	b	c	d	e

28

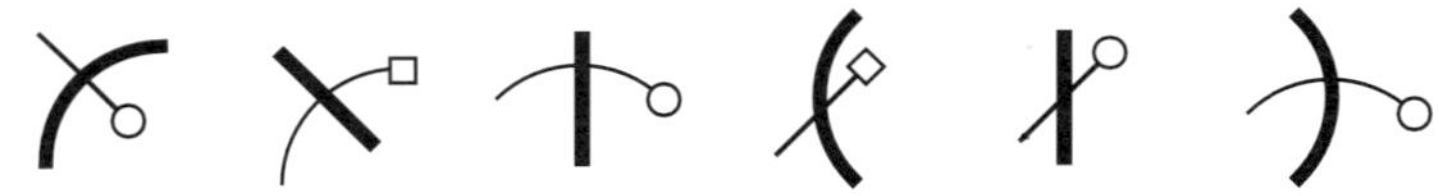

AR BU BS AT BR ?

AR	BT	AS	BR	AT
a	b	c	d	e

29

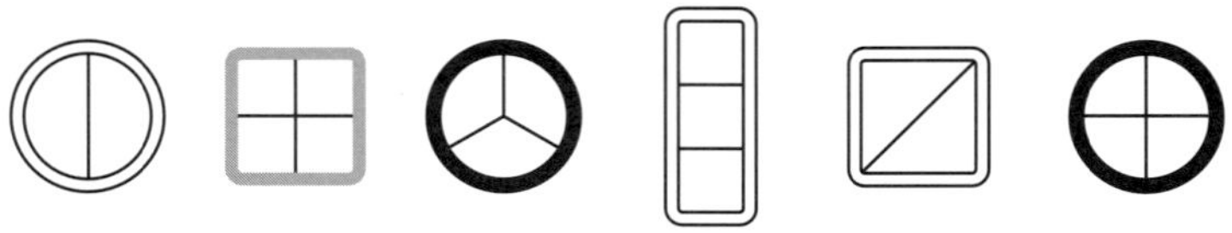

DC GA EB FB FC ?

EA	FA	GB	DC	EB
a	b	c	d	e

30

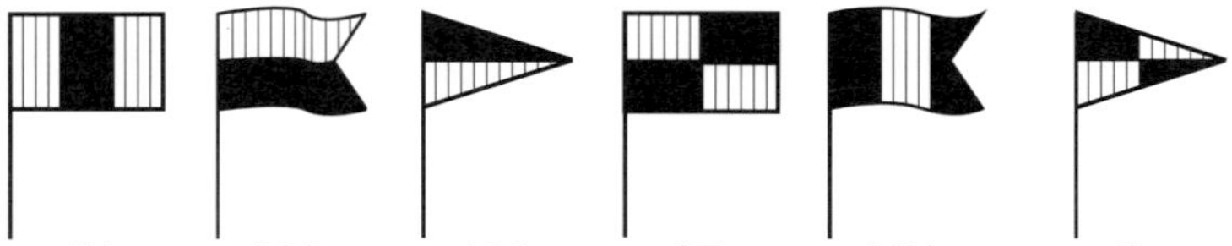

JX KY LY JZ KX ?

LX	JY	KZ	JX	LZ
a	b	c	d	e

Find the shape or pattern which completes the square. Circle the letter.

Example

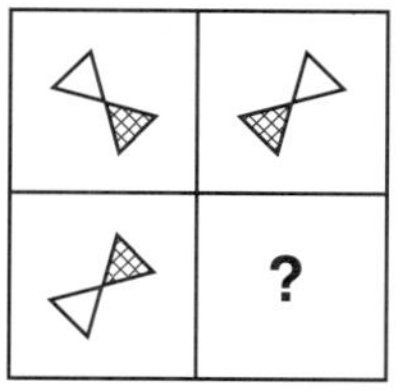

a b c d e

31

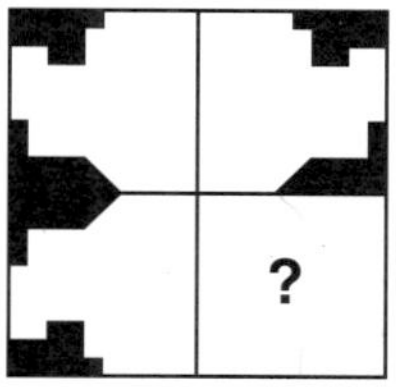

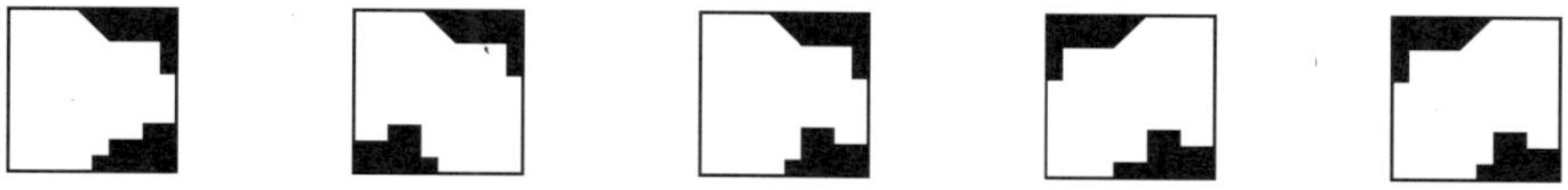

a b c d e

32

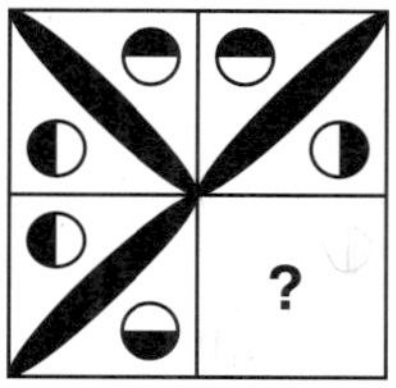

a b c d e

33

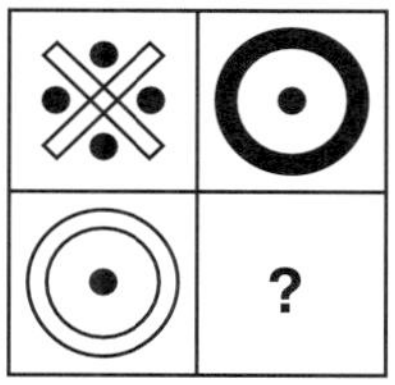

a b c d e

34

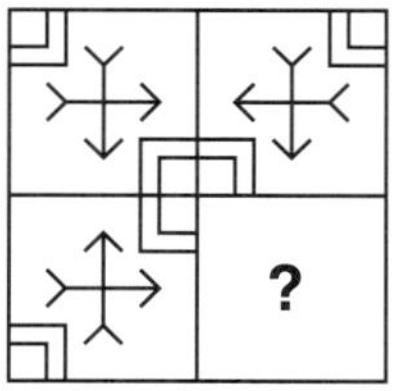

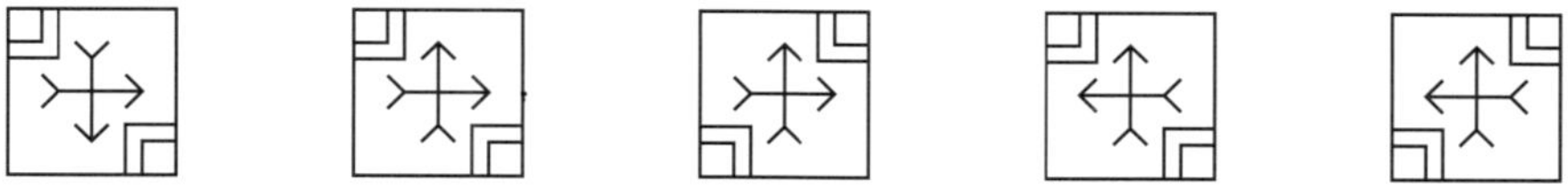

a b c d e

35

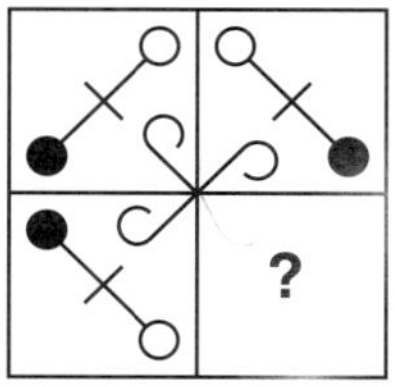

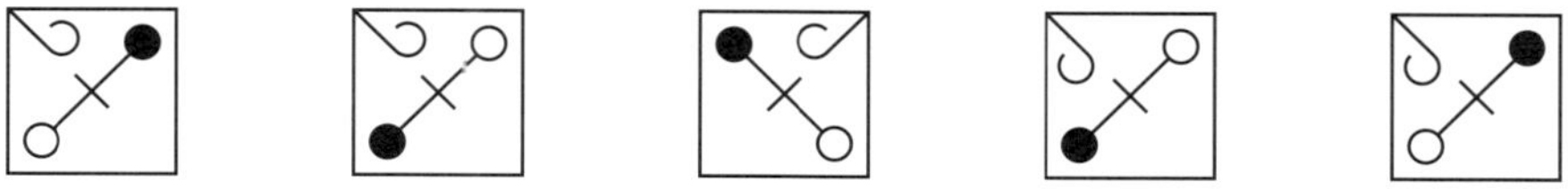

a b c d e

36

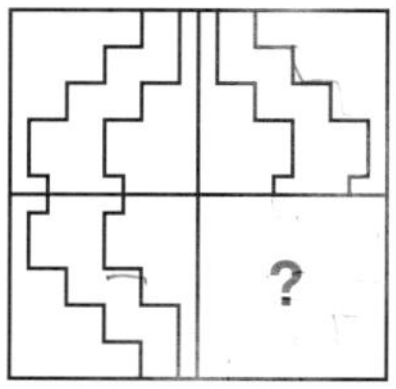

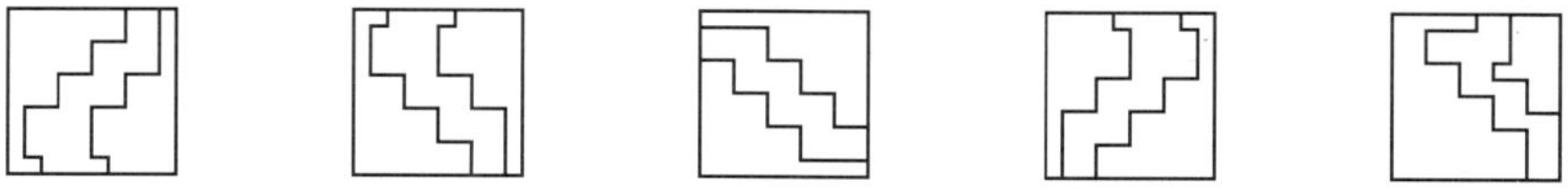

a b c d e

37

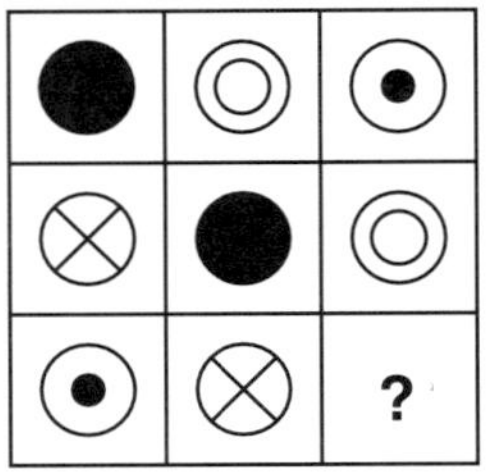

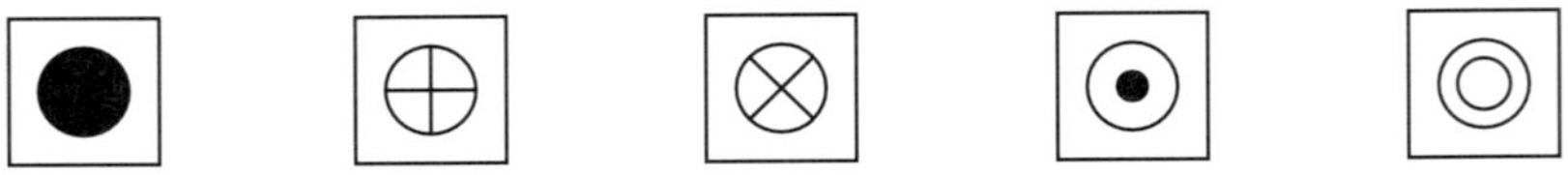

a b c d e

38

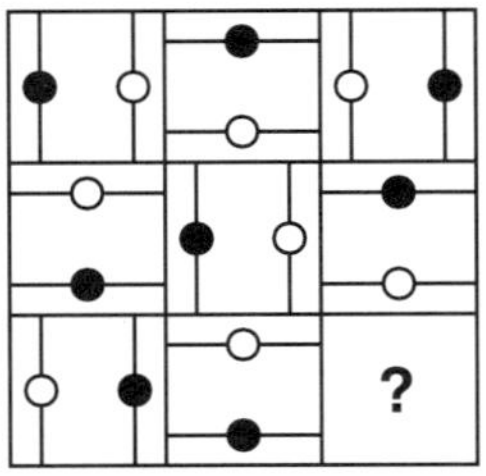

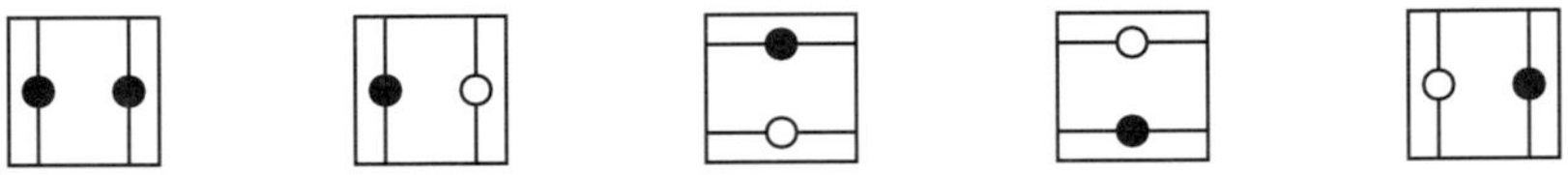

a b c d e

39

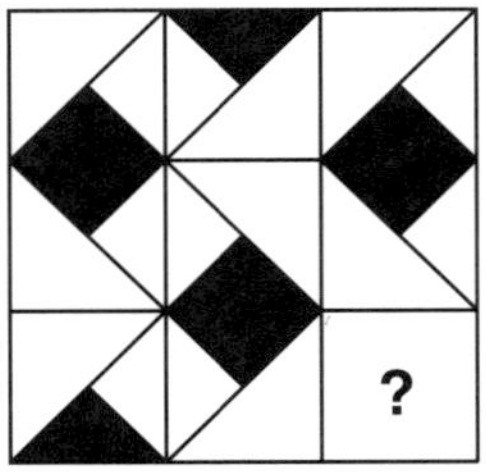

a b c d e

40

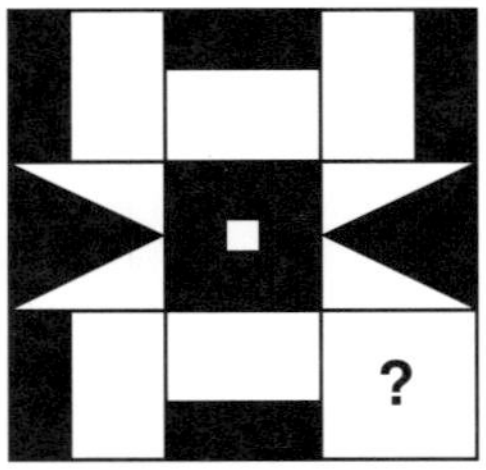

a b c d e

41

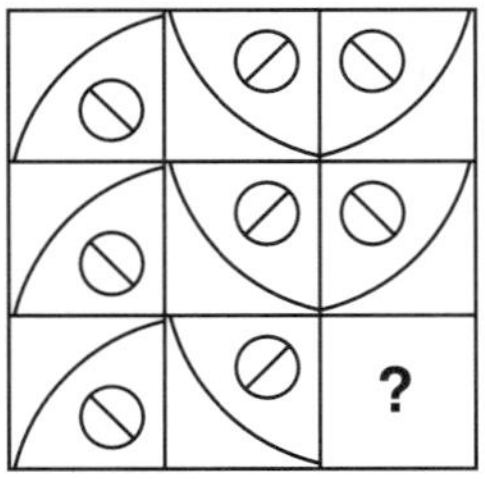

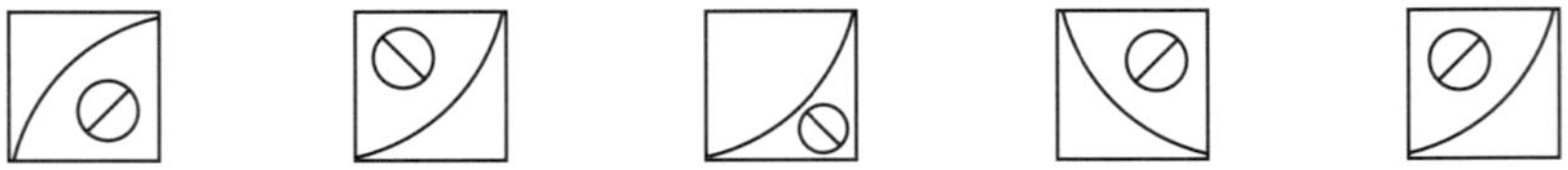

a b c d e

42

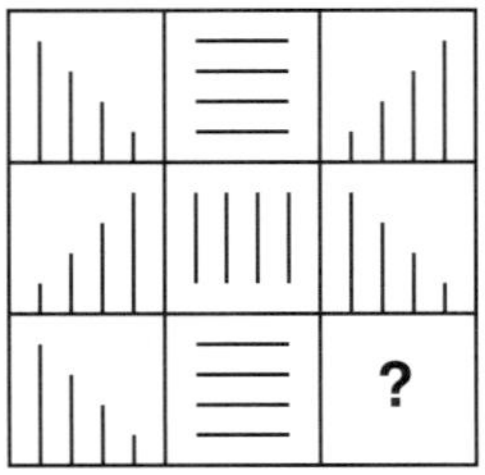

a b c d e

Which shape or pattern is made when the first two shapes or patterns are put together?

Example

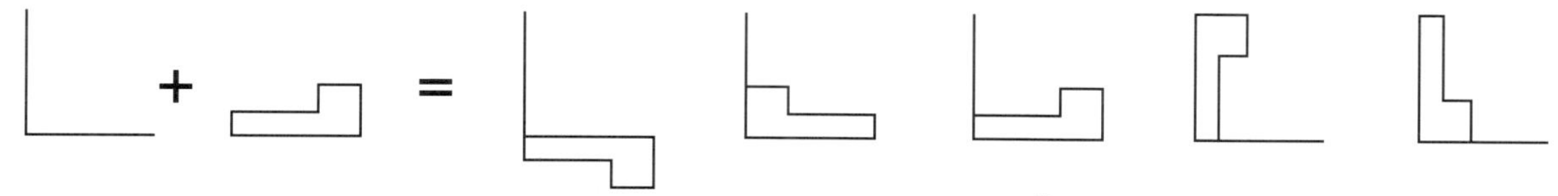

a b c d e

43

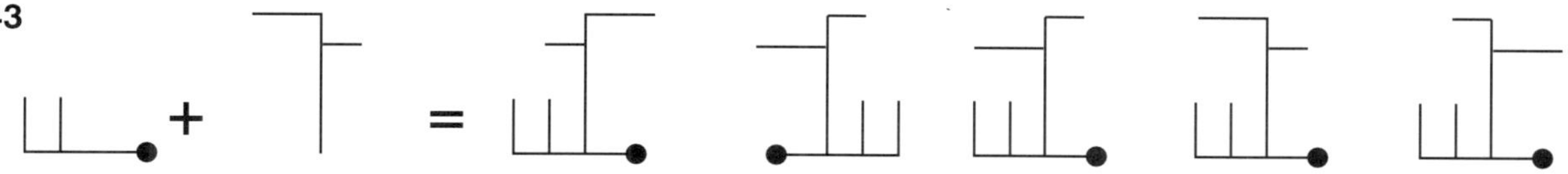

a b c d e

44

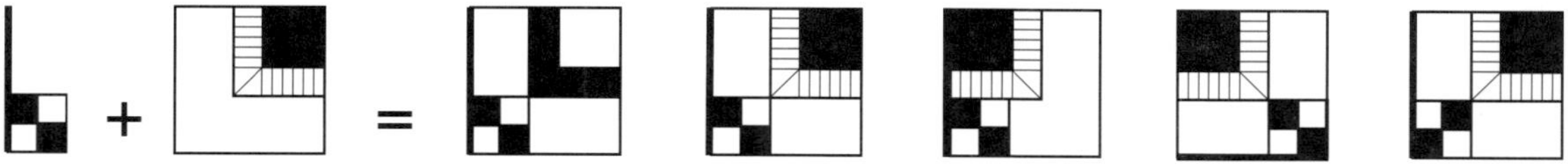

a b c d e

45

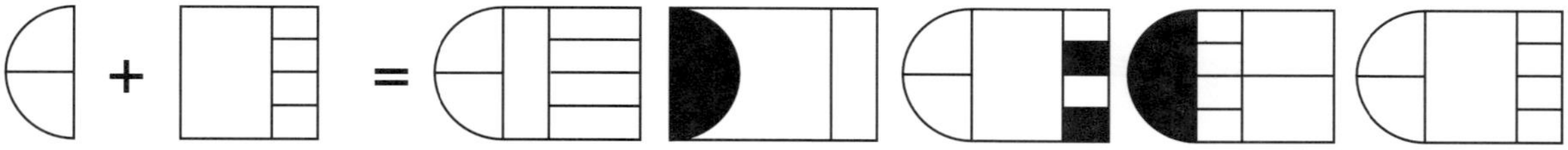

a b c d e

46

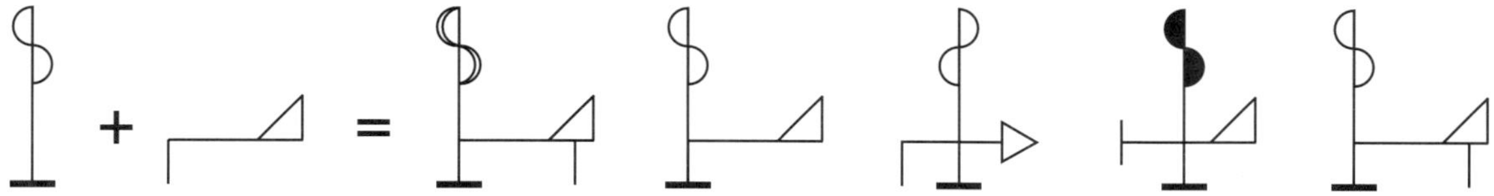

a b c d e

47

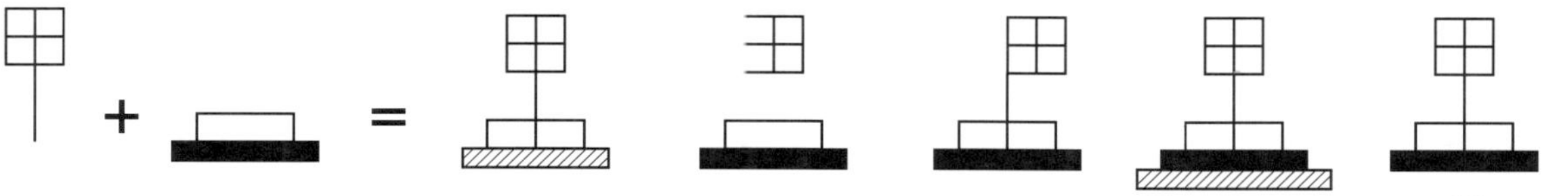

a b c d e

48

a b c d e

Find the shape or pattern which completes the second pair in the same way as the first pair. Circle the letter.

Example

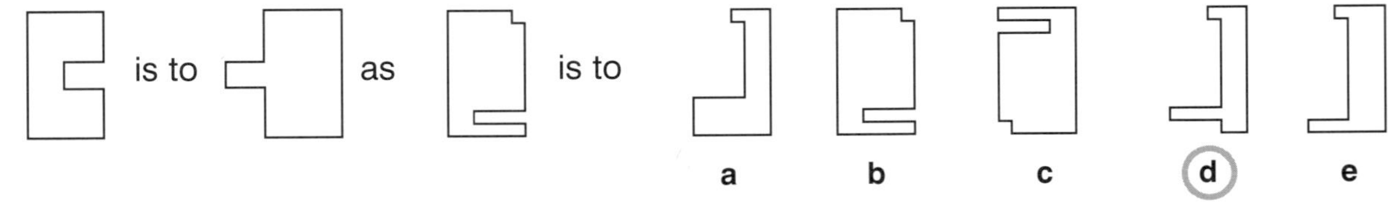

49
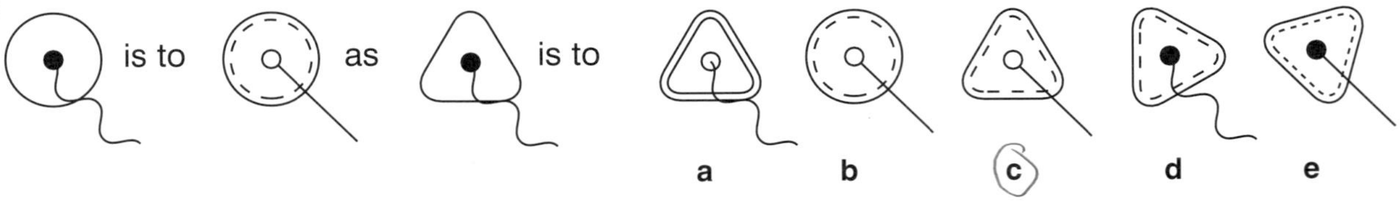

50
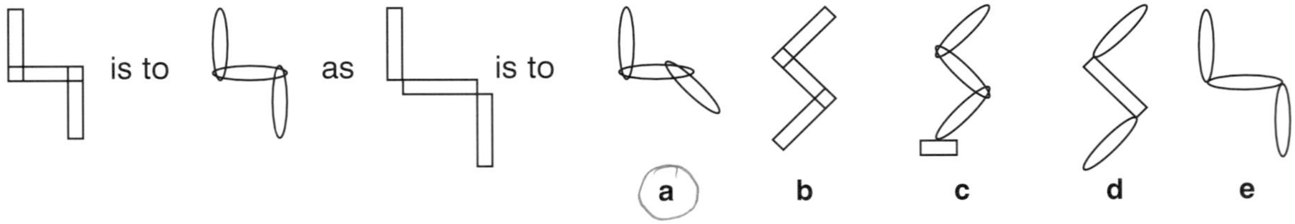

51
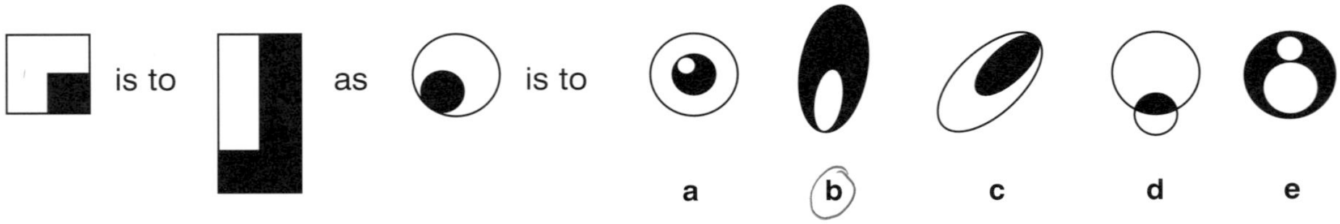

52
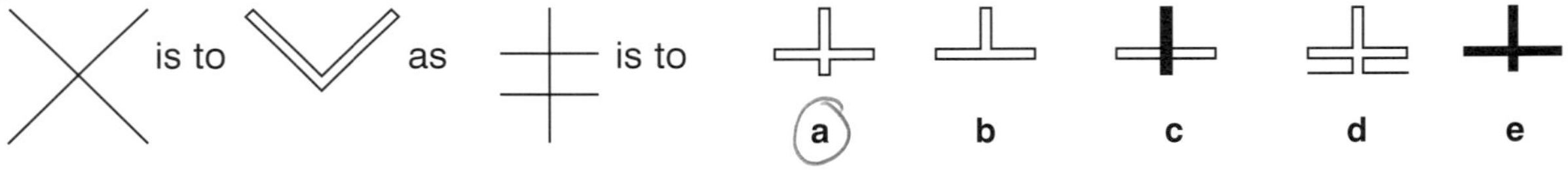

53
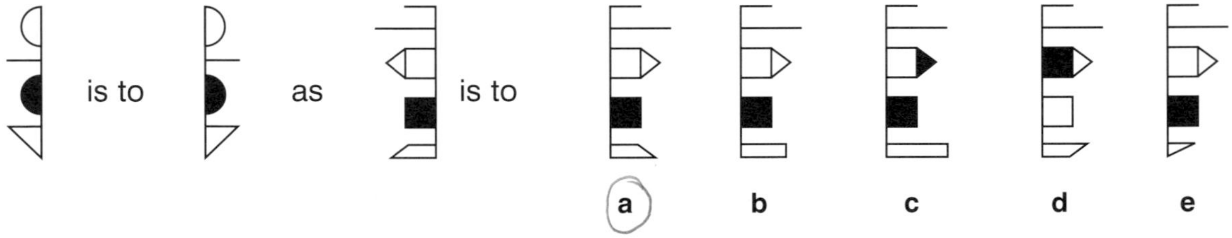

54
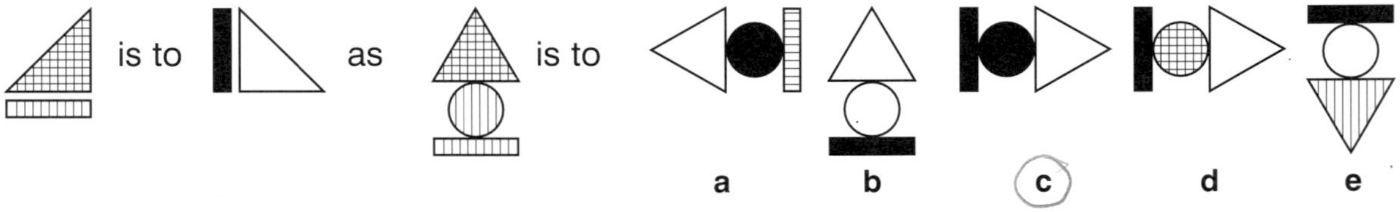

55
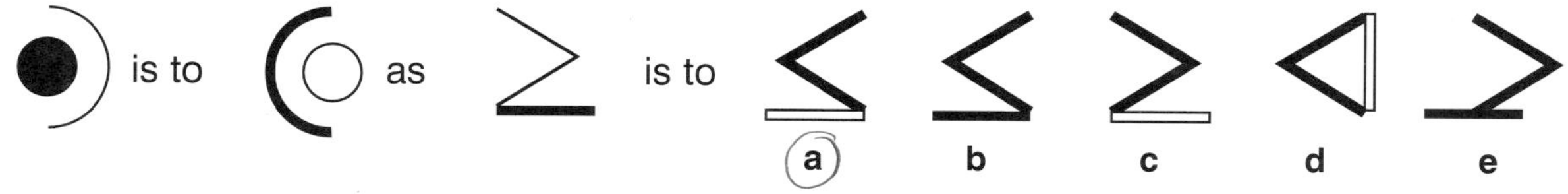

56
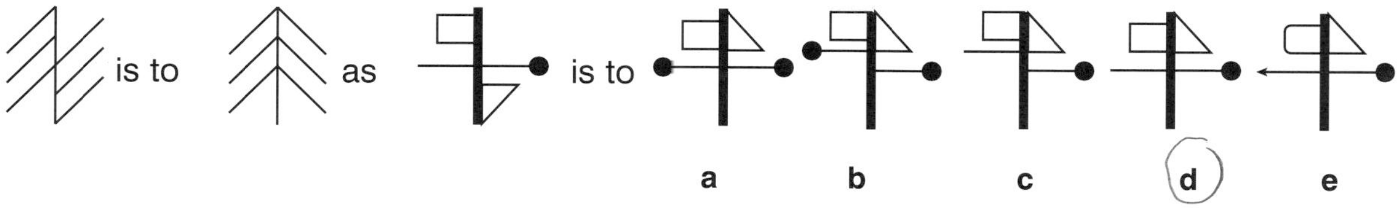

57
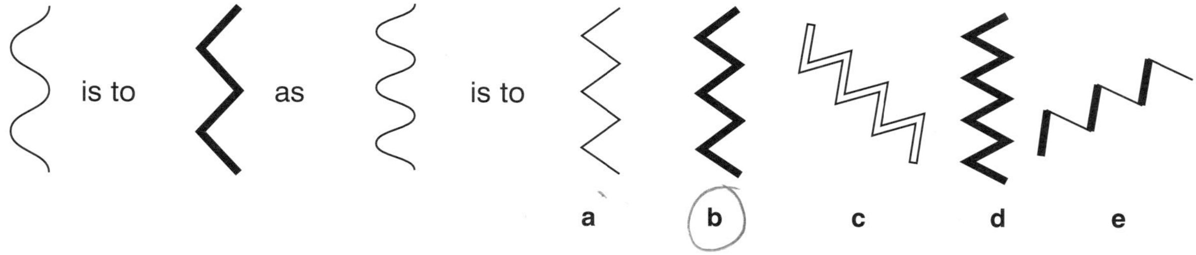

58
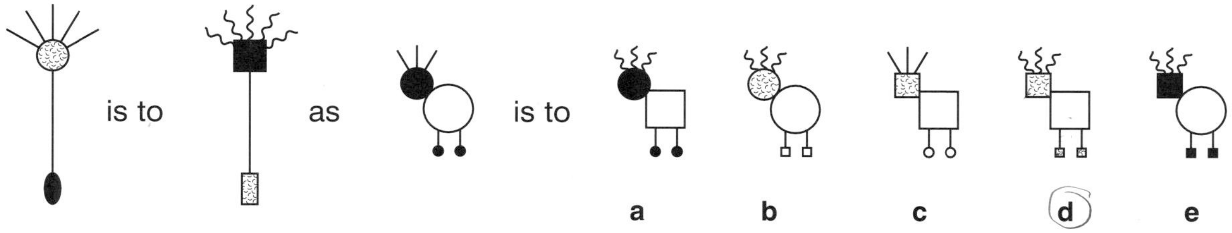

59
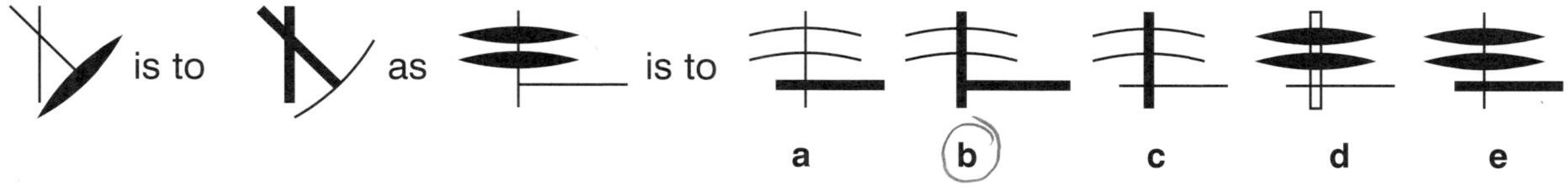

60
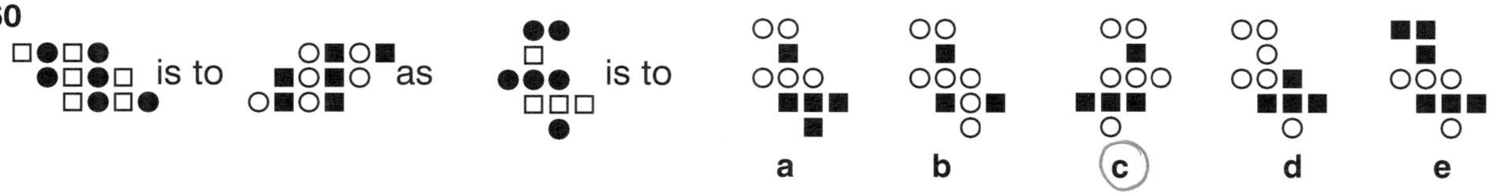

Paper 4

Which shape is most similar to the shapes in the group on the left? Circle the letter.

Example

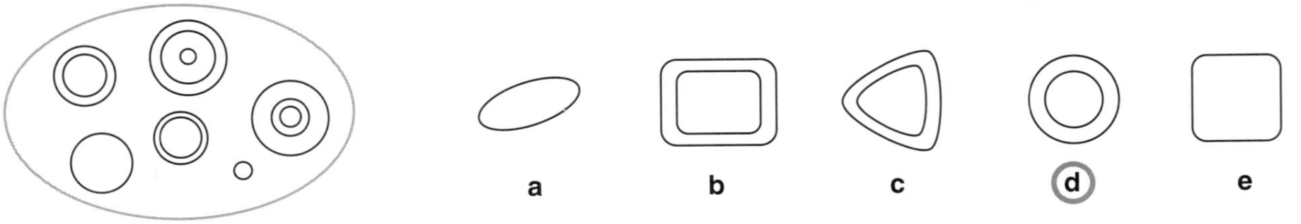

a b c d e

1

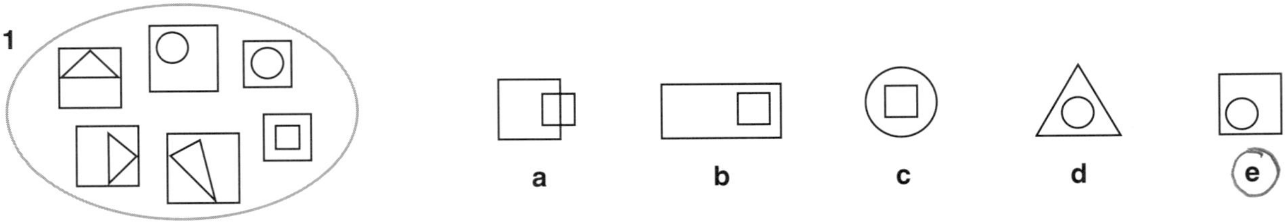

a b c d e

2

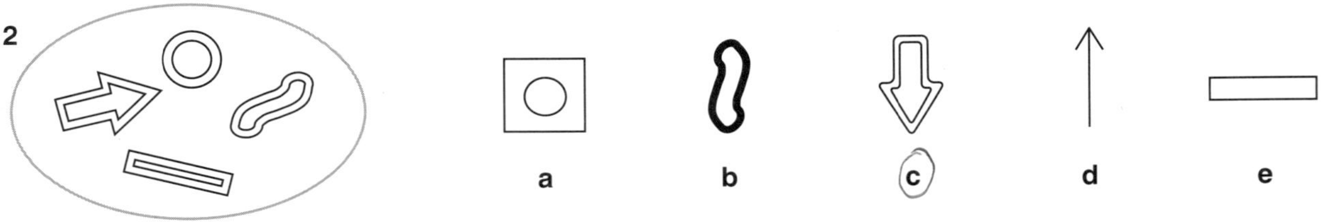

a b c d e

3

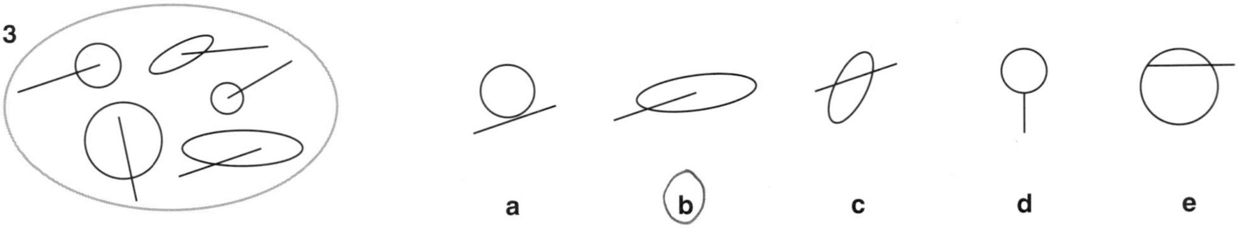

a b c d e

4

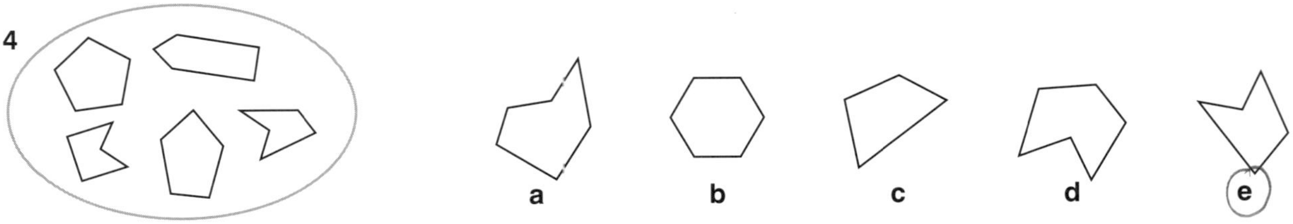

a b c d e

5

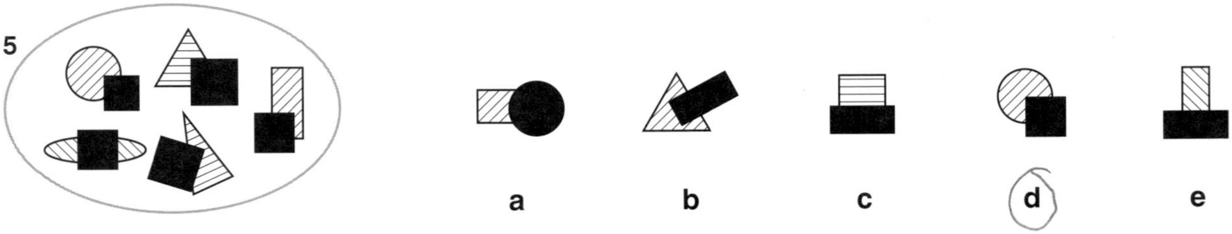

a b c d e

Paper 1

1	a	31	c
2	b	32	d
3	c	33	d
4	e	34	d
5	c	35	c
6	a	36	b
7	a	37	e
8	c	38	b
9	d	39	b
10	e	40	a
11	b	41	d
12	a	42	c
13	d	43	d
14	d	44	e
15	e	45	d
16	b	46	b
17	e	47	c
18	a	48	b
19	d	49	e
20	c	50	e
21	a	51	b
22	e	52	d
23	b	53	e
24	b	54	c
25	e	55	c
26	b	56	a
27	c	57	e
28	e	58	d
29	c	59	e
30	a	60	d

Paper 2

1	b	31	d
2	c	32	d
3	b	33	e
4	a	34	c
5	a	35	d
6	c	36	d
7	b	37	e
8	d	38	e
9	b	39	c
10	a	40	c
11	c	41	a
12	d	42	d
13	c	43	d
14	e	44	d
15	c	45	c
16	b	46	b
17	b	47	e
18	e	48	e
19	a	49	a
20	a	50	c
21	c	51	d
22	a	52	c
23	d	53	e
24	a	54	d
25	b	55	b
26	e	56	d
27	b	57	e
28	d	58	c
29	e	59	d
30	b	60	e

Answers

Paper 3

1	c	31	c
2	e	32	a
3	e	33	c
4	b	34	d
5	b	35	e
6	a	36	d
7	d	37	a
8	c	38	b
9	e	39	b
10	d	40	c
11	e	41	b
12	c	42	e
13	e	43	d
14	b	44	b
15	d	45	e
16	e	46	b
17	c	47	e
18	b	48	d
19	c	49	c
20	d	50	e
21	e	51	b
22	d	52	a
23	b	53	a
24	e	54	c
25	d	55	a
26	c	56	d
27	d	57	b
28	c	58	d
29	a	59	b
30	e	60	c

Paper 4

1	e	31	d
2	c	32	c
3	b	33	a
4	e	34	d
5	d	35	b
6	b	36	d
7	d	37	a
8	c	38	a
9	e	39	d
10	a	40	e
11	a	41	b
12	b	42	e
13	c	43	d
14	d	44	d
15	b	45	c
16	c	46	b
17	b	47	e
18	a	48	e
19	e	49	a
20	a	50	a
21	b	51	c
22	e	52	a
23	d	53	b
24	e	54	d
25	b	55	a
26	c	56	c
27	e	57	b
28	c	58	c
29	d	59	a
30	d	60	c

Paper 5

1	c	31	e
2	d	32	d
3	e	33	d
4	a	34	c
5	b	35	c
6	b	36	a
7	d	37	c
8	c	38	e
9	d	39	b
10	c	40	d
11	c	41	e
12	a	42	c
13	b	43	a
14	c	44	e
15	d	45	c
16	b	46	d
17	e	47	b
18	d	48	e
19	c	49	a
20	c	50	e
21	d	51	c
22	e	52	e
23	b	53	d
24	c	54	e
25	a	55	c
26	a	56	e
27	e	57	d
28	a	58	d
29	b	59	d
30	d	60	b

Paper 6

1	b	31	b
2	c	32	c
3	e	33	d
4	b	34	c
5	c	35	c
6	d	36	d
7	b	37	a
8	a	38	b
9	a	39	e
10	b	40	a
11	c	41	d
12	e	42	e
13	c	43	b
14	d	44	b
15	e	45	e
16	c	46	c
17	b	47	a
18	e	48	e
19	d	49	e
20	e	50	d
21	d	51	e
22	b	52	e
23	d	53	c
24	b	54	c
25	a	55	e
26	d	56	d
27	b	57	d
28	d	58	a
29	c	59	b
30	e	60	a

6

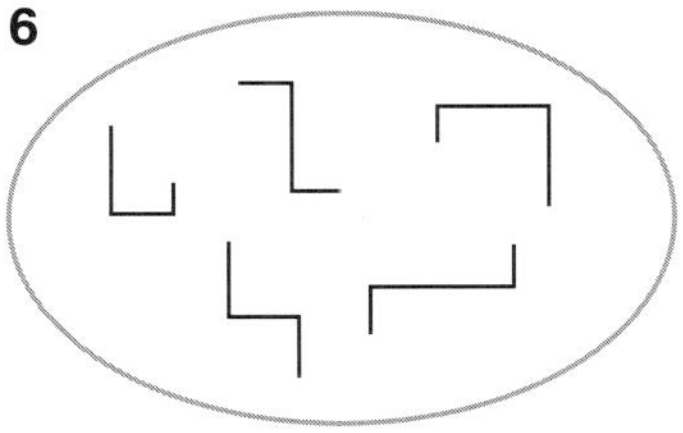

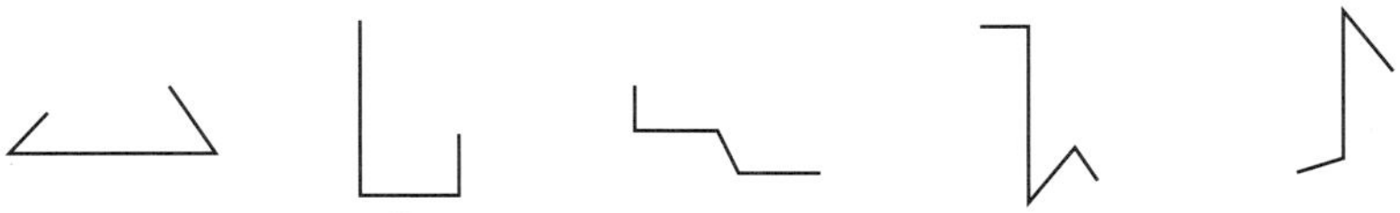

a b c d e

7

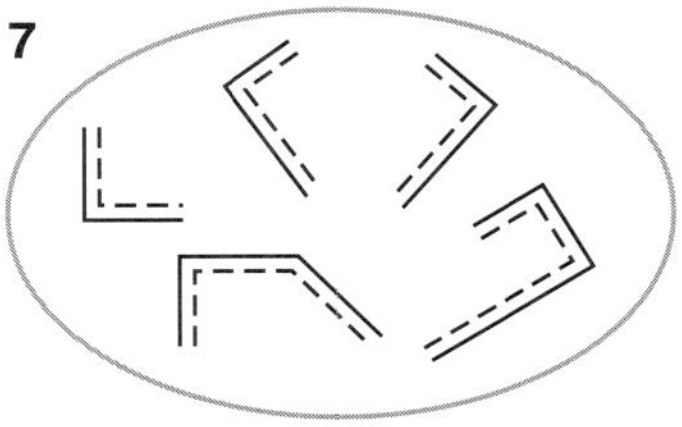

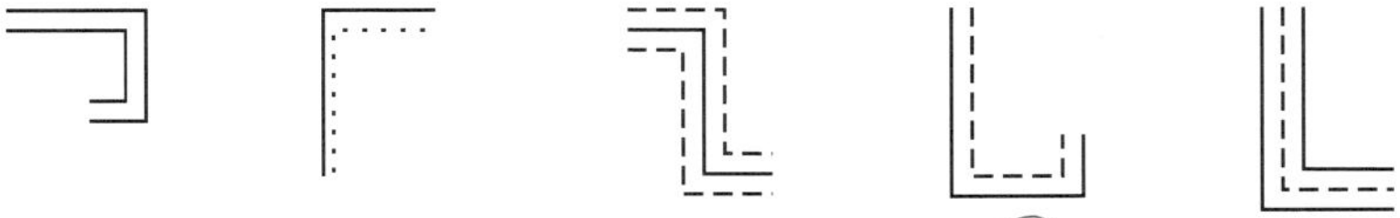

a b c d e

8

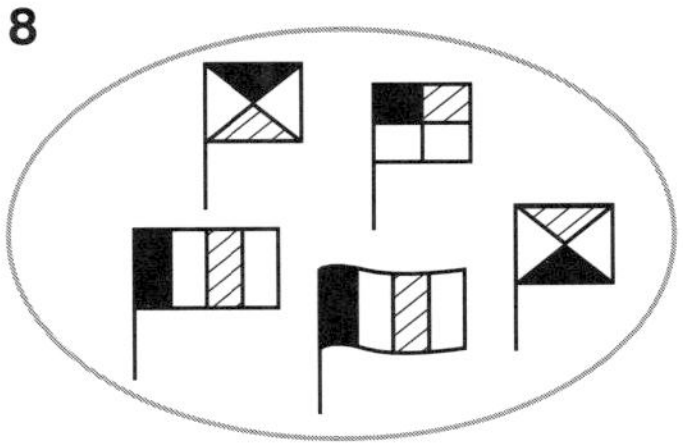

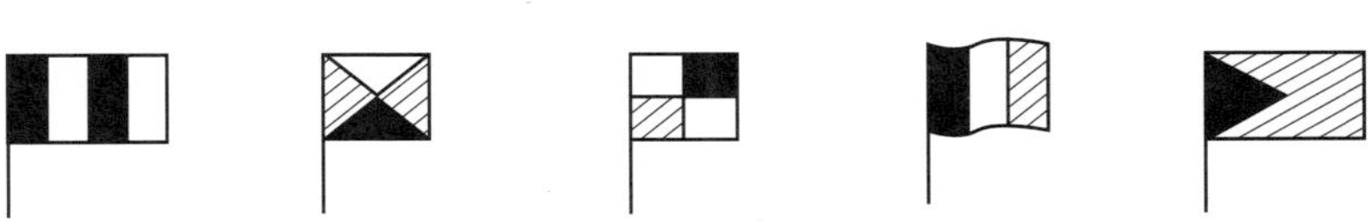

a b c d e

9

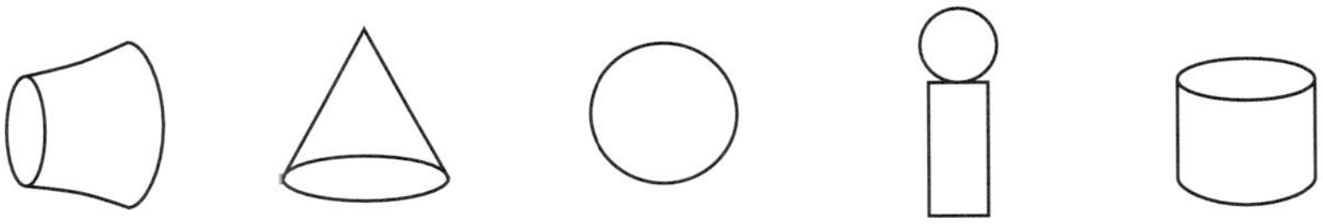

a b c d e

10

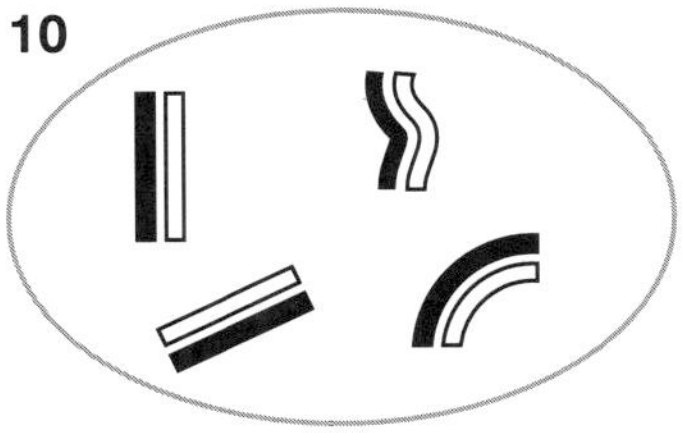

a b c d e

11

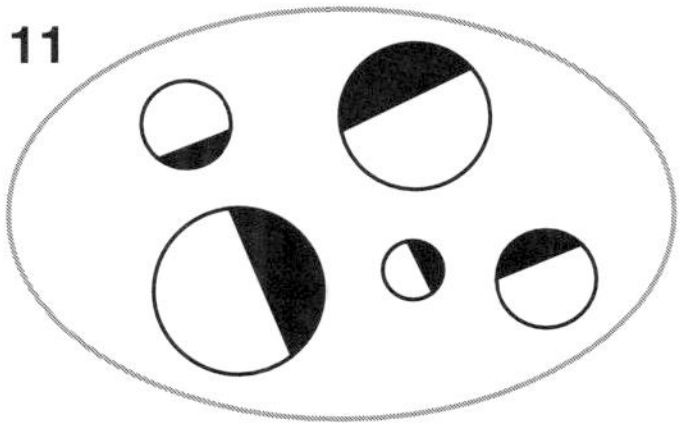

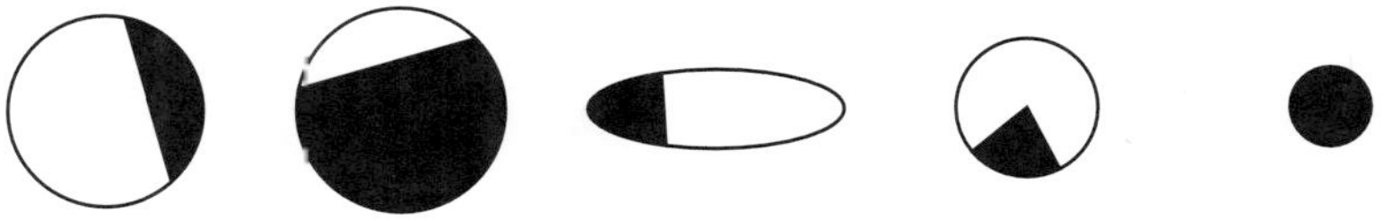

a b c d e

12

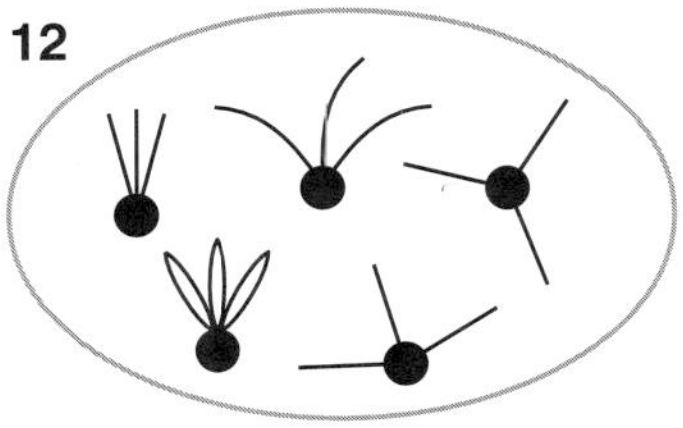

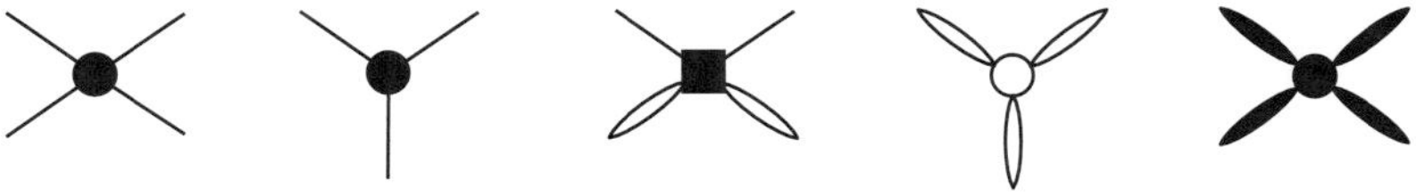

a b c d e

Find the shape or pattern which completes or continues the given series. Circle the letter.

Example

a b c d e

13

a b c d e

14

a b c d e

15

a b c d e

16

a b c d e

17

a b c d e

18

a b c d e

19

a b c d e

20

a b c d e

21

a b c d e

22

a b c d e

23

a b c d e

24

a b c d e

Which shape on the right is the reflection of the shape given on the left? Circle the letter.

Example

a b c d e

25

a b c d e

26

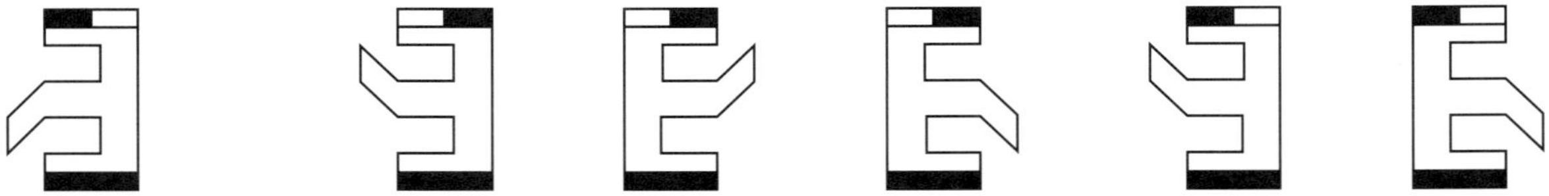

a b c d e

27

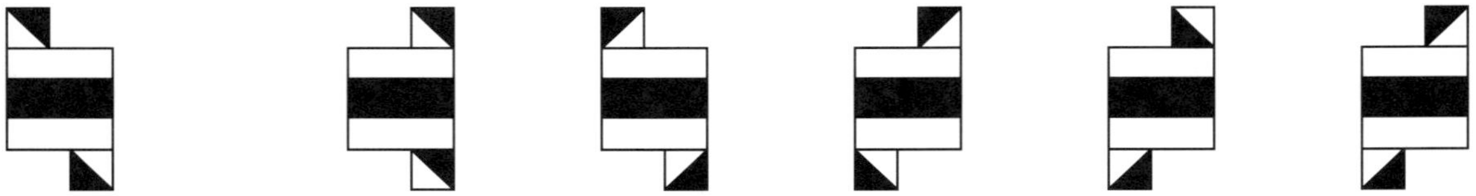

a b c d e

28

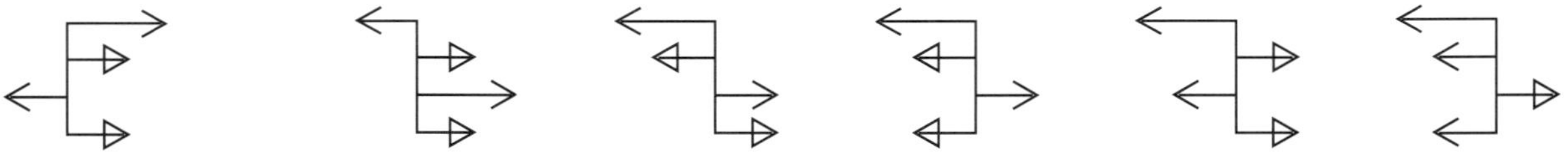

a b c d e

29

a b c d e

30

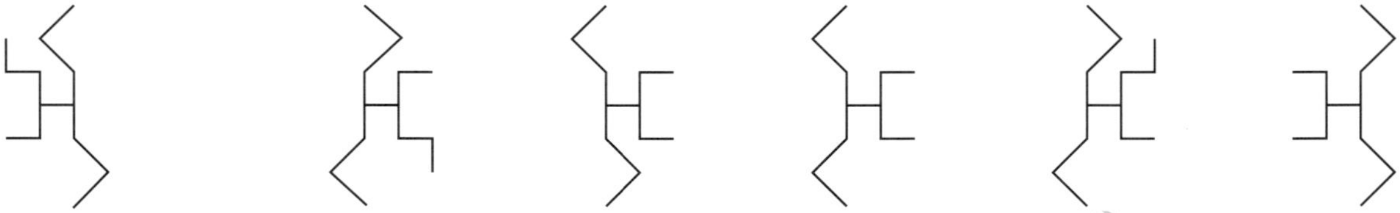

a b c d e

Find the shape or pattern which completes the second pair in the same way as the first pair. Circle the letter.

Example

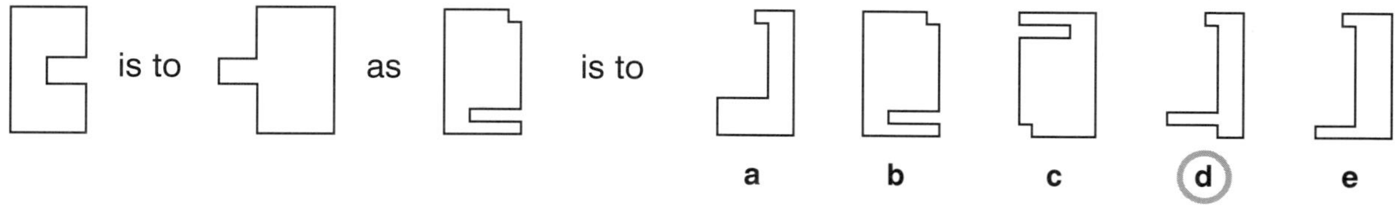

31

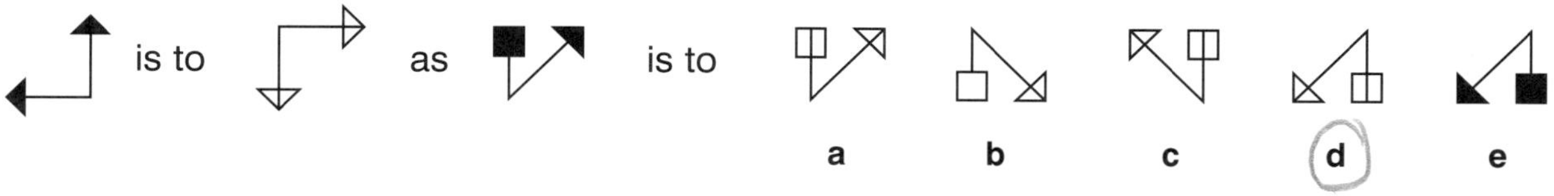

32

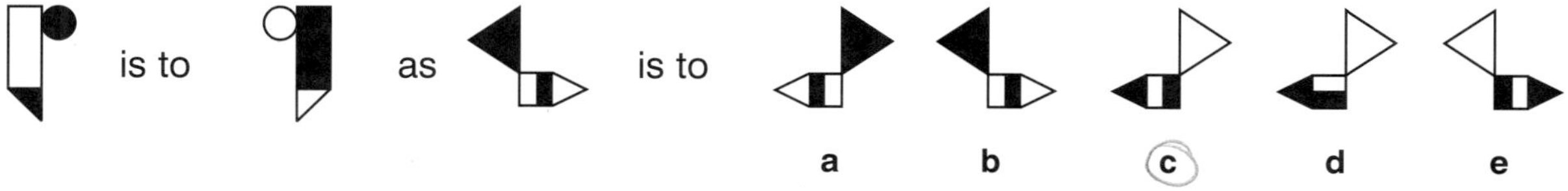

33

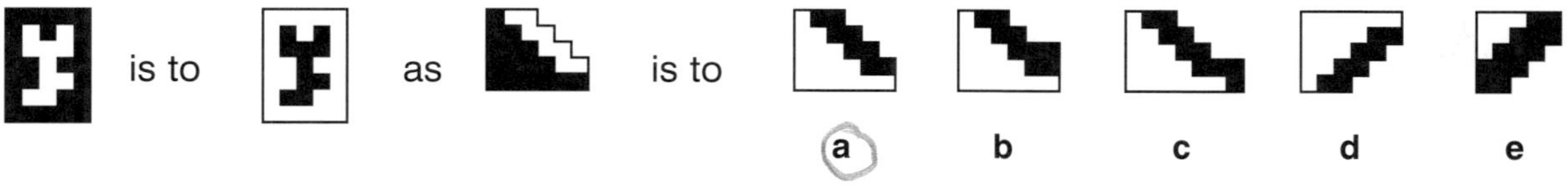

34

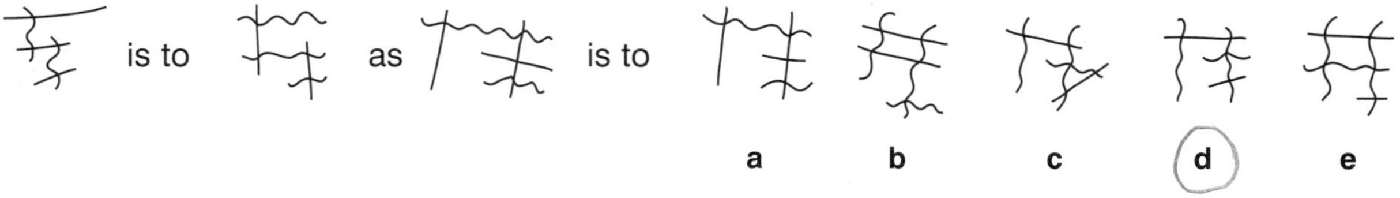

35

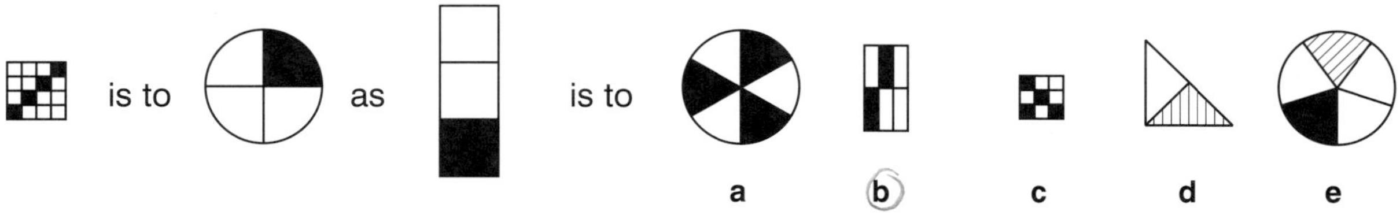

36

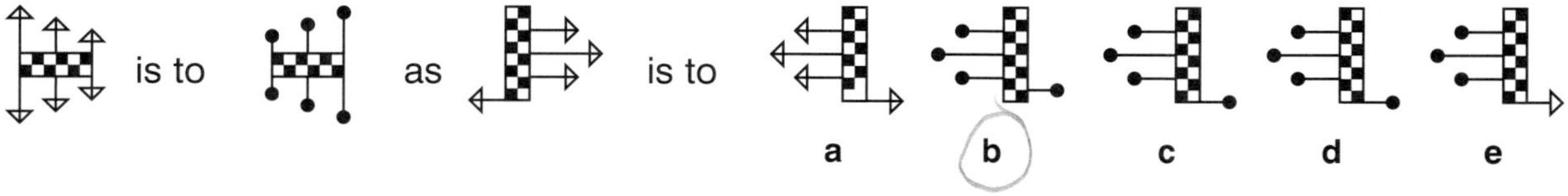

37

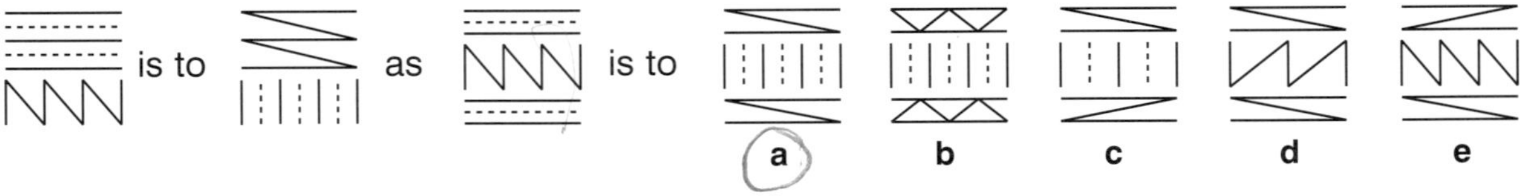

38

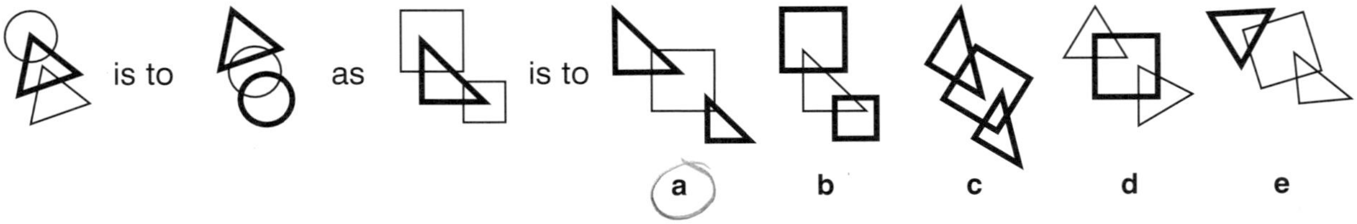

39

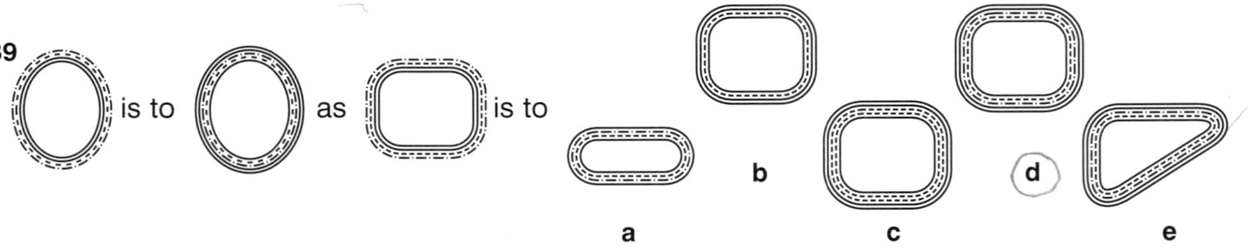

40

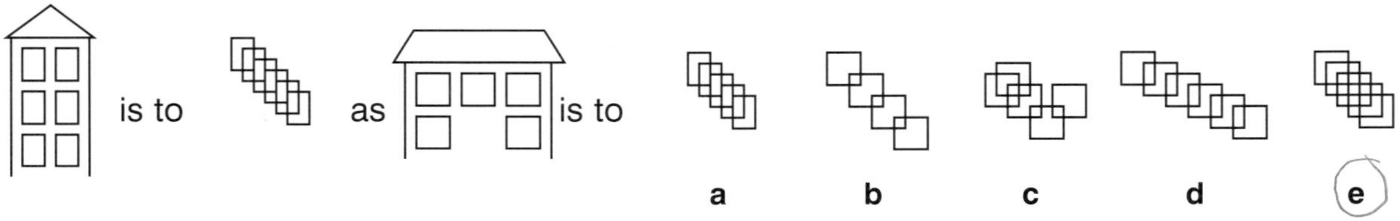

41

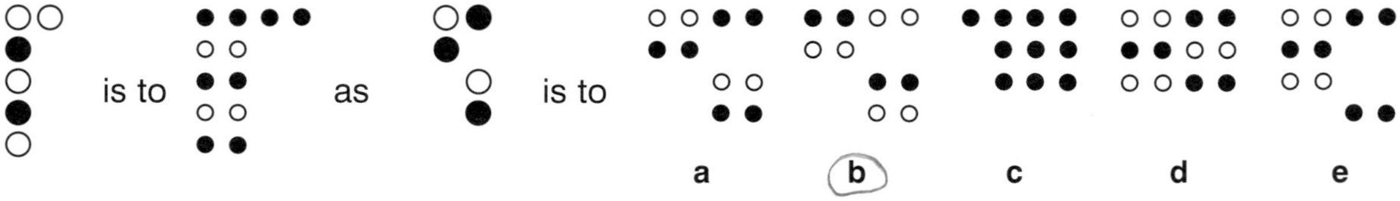

42

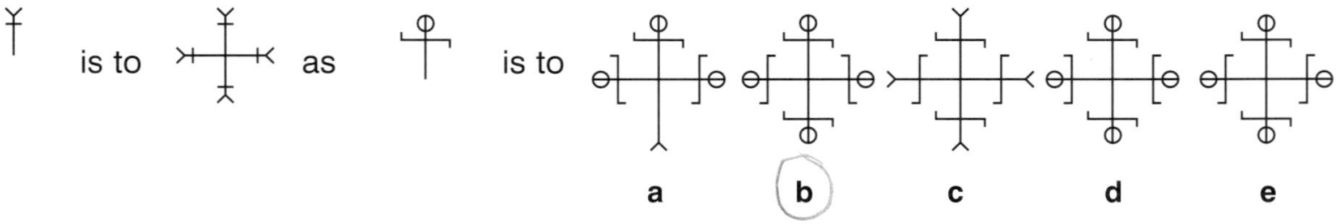

Find the shape or pattern which completes the square. Circle the letter.

Example

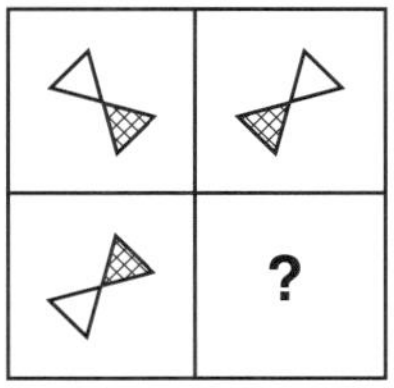

a b c d e

43

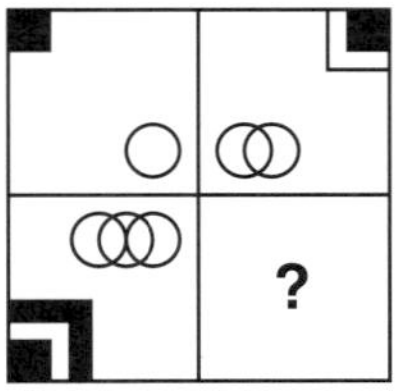

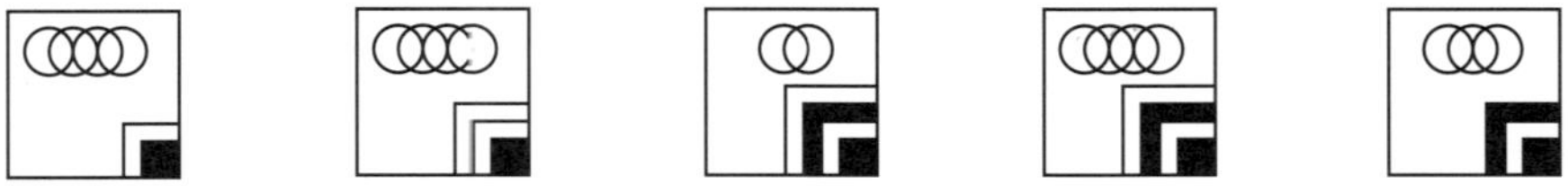

a b c d e

44

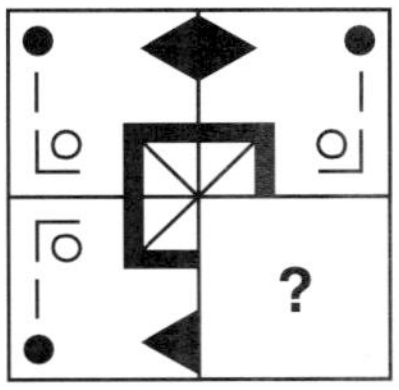

a b c d e

45

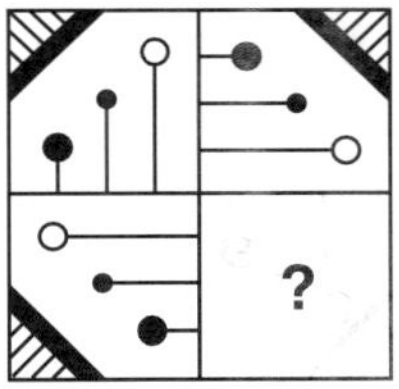

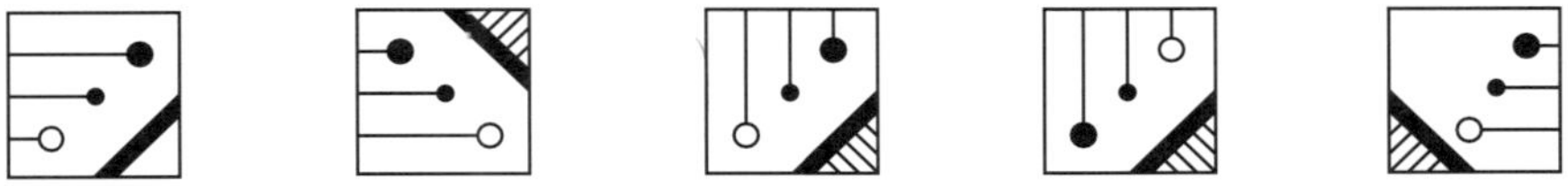

a b c d e

46

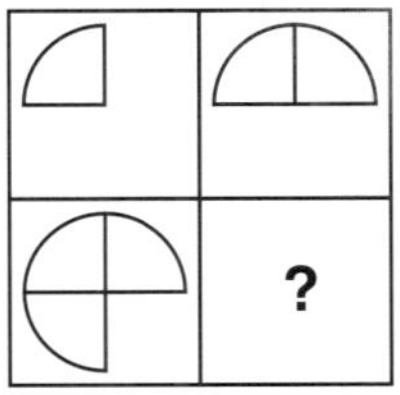

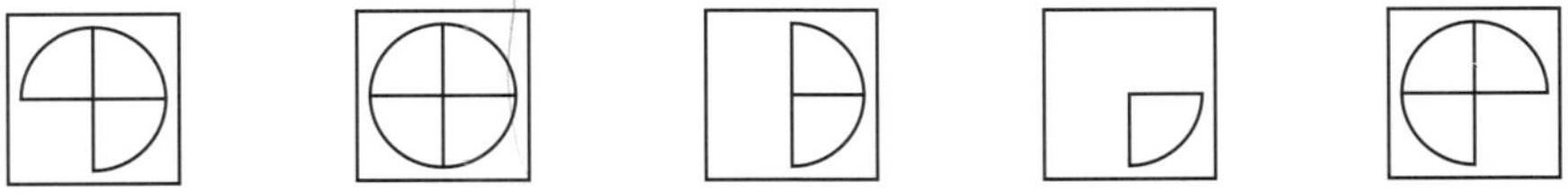

a b c d e

47

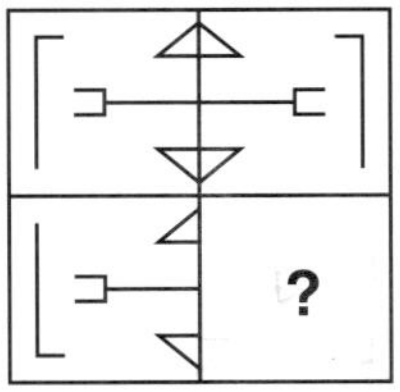

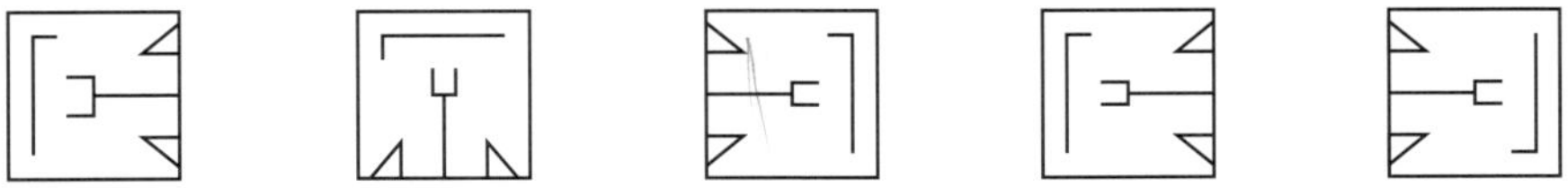

a b c d e

48

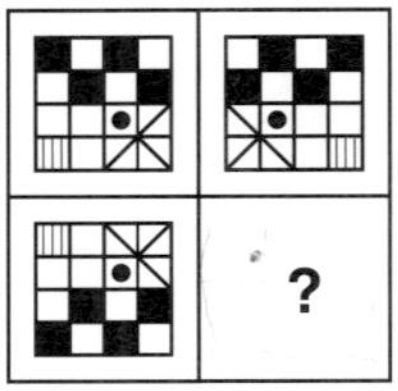

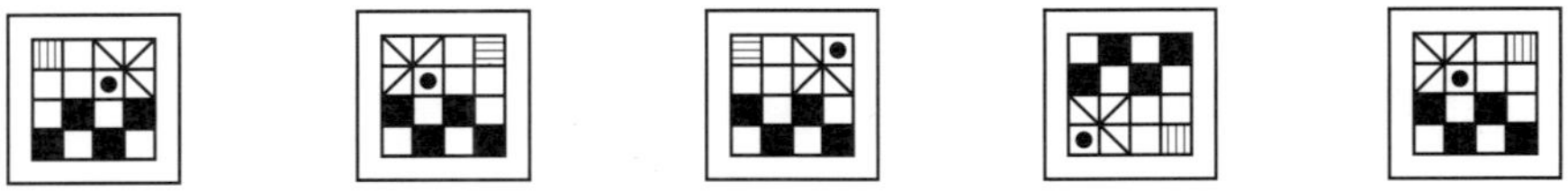

a b c d e

49 

a b c d e

50 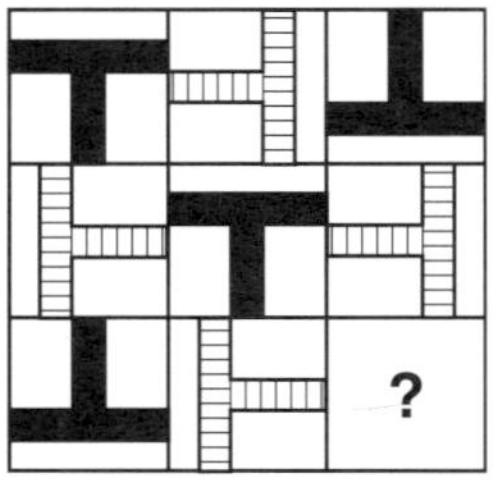

a b c d e

51 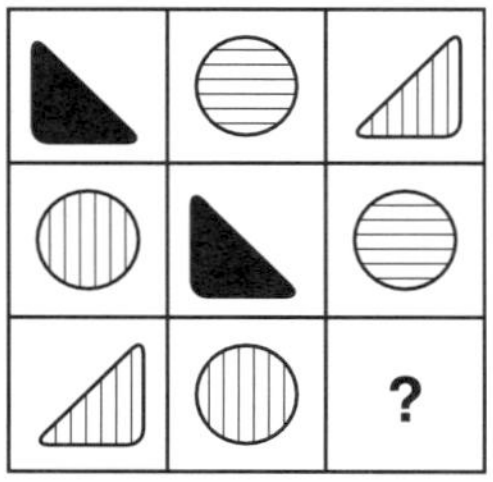

a b c d e

52 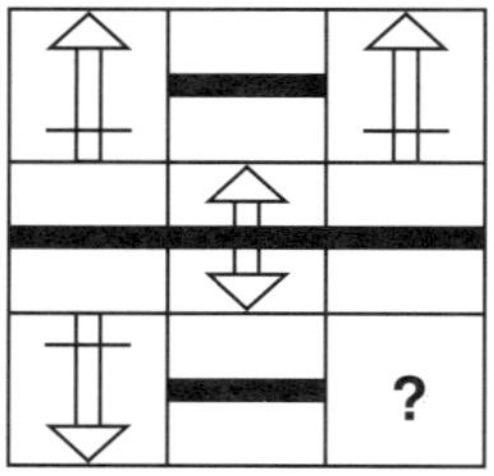

a b c d e

53 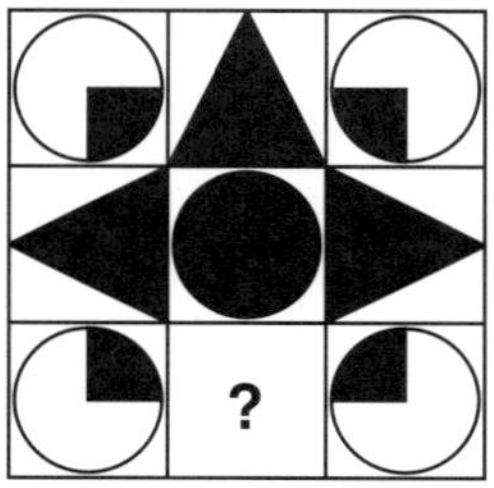

a b c d e

54 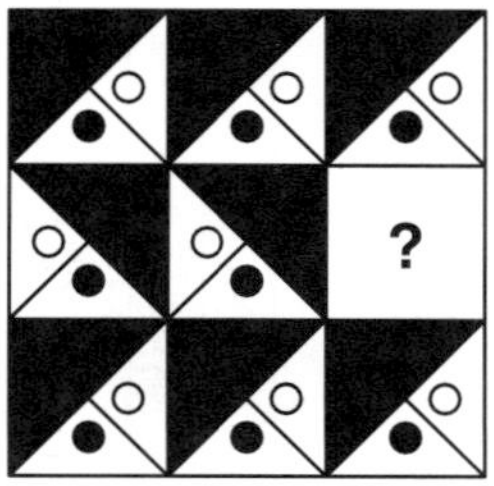

a b c d e

Which cube could not be made from the given net? Circle the letter.

Example

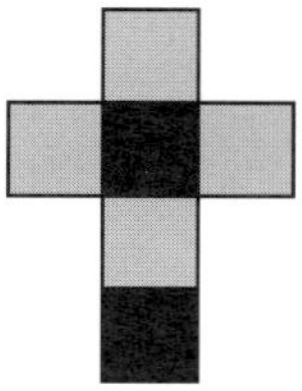

a b c d e

55

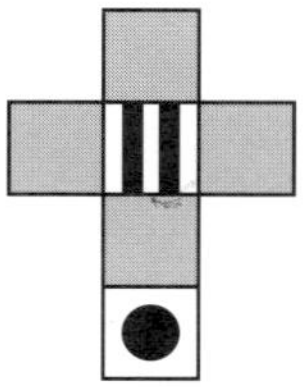

a b c d e

56

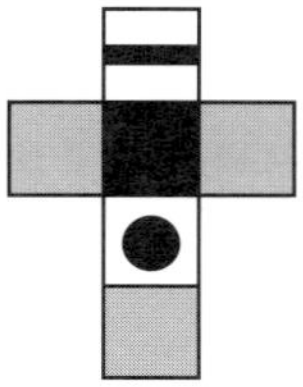

a b c d e

57

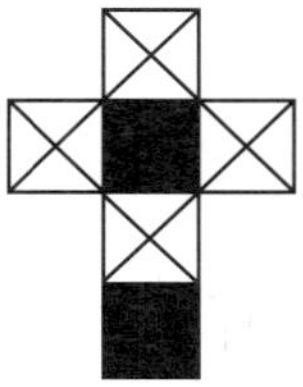

a b c d e

58

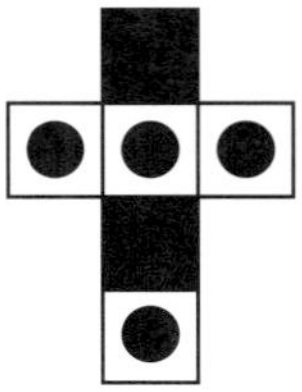

a b c d e

59

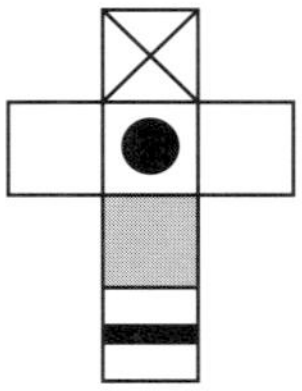

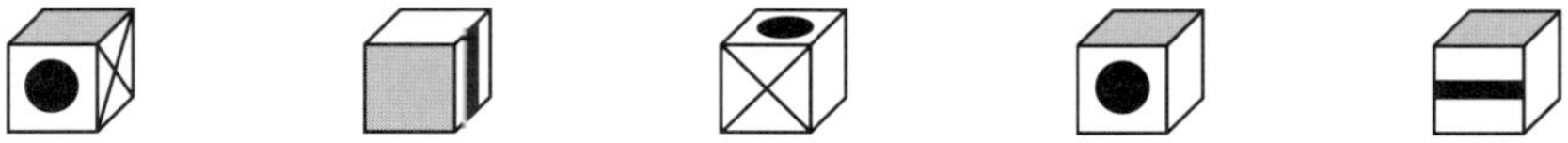

a b c d e

60

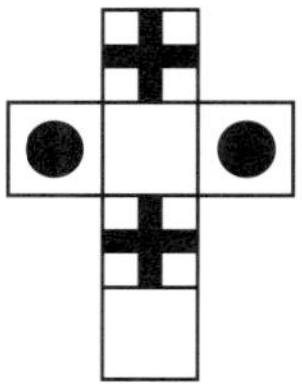

a b c d e

Paper 5

Find the shape or pattern which completes or continues the given series. Circle the letter.

Example

a b (c) d e

1

a b c d e

2

a b c d e

3

a b c d e

4

a b c d e

5

a b c d e

6

a b c d e

7

a b c d e

8

a b c d e

9

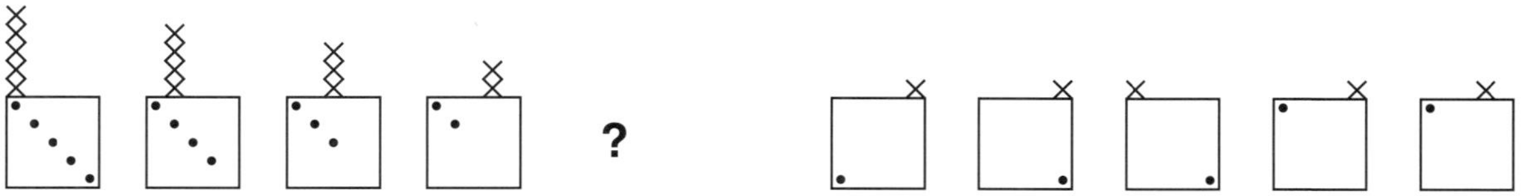

a b c d e

10

a b c d e

11

a b c d e

12

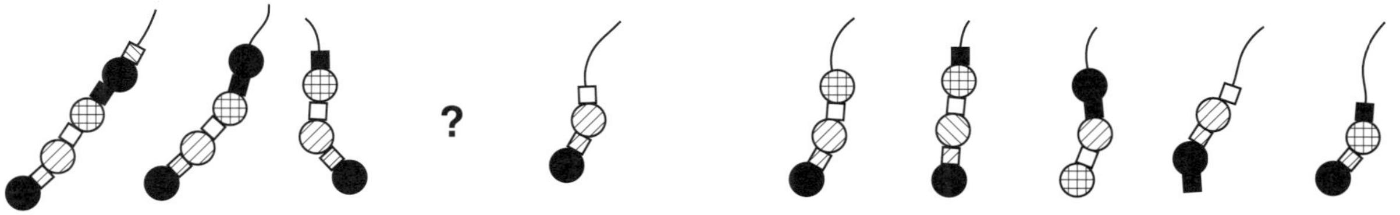

a b c d e

Find the shape or pattern which completes the second pair in the same way as the first pair. Circle the letter.

Example

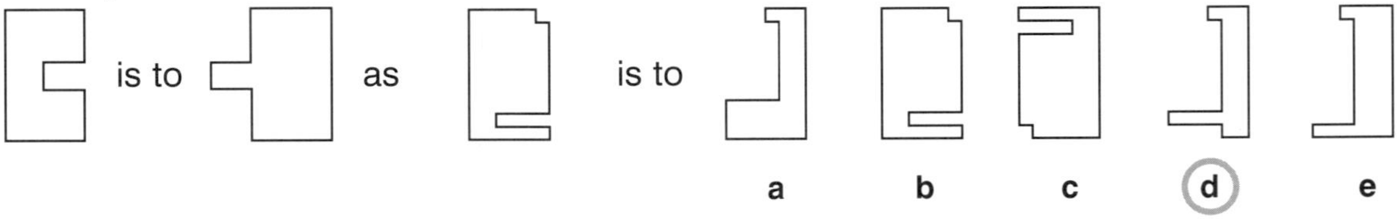

13

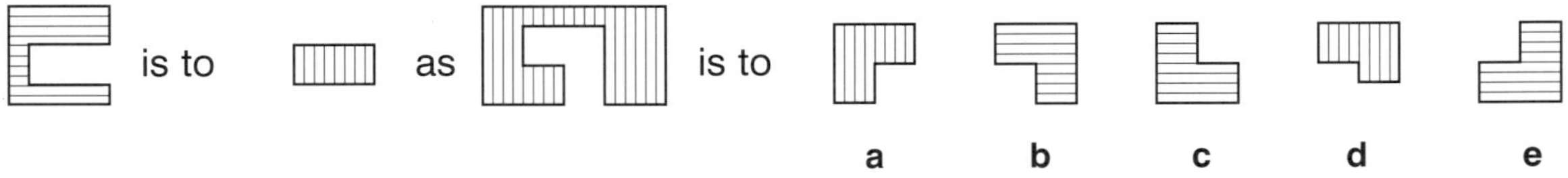

14

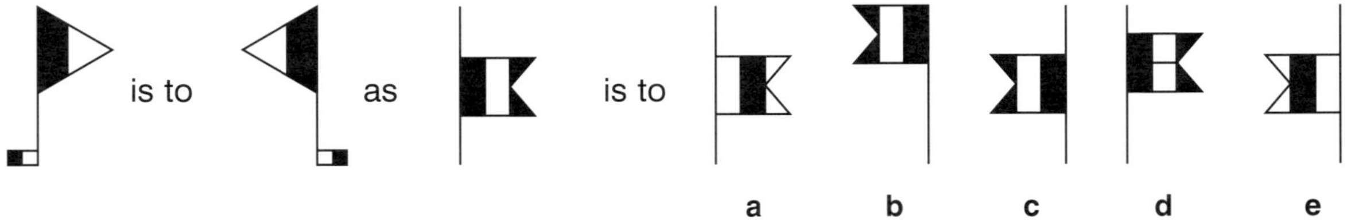

15

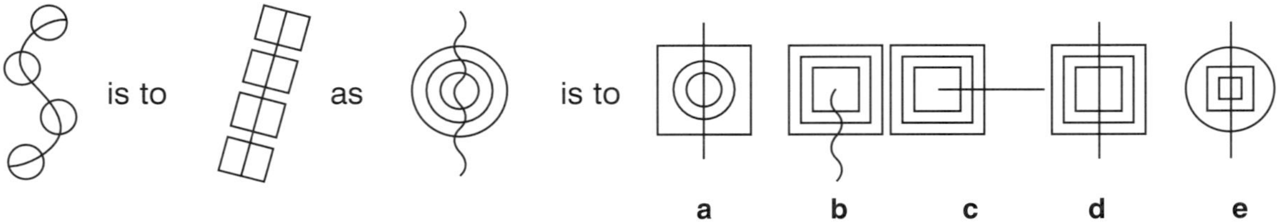

16

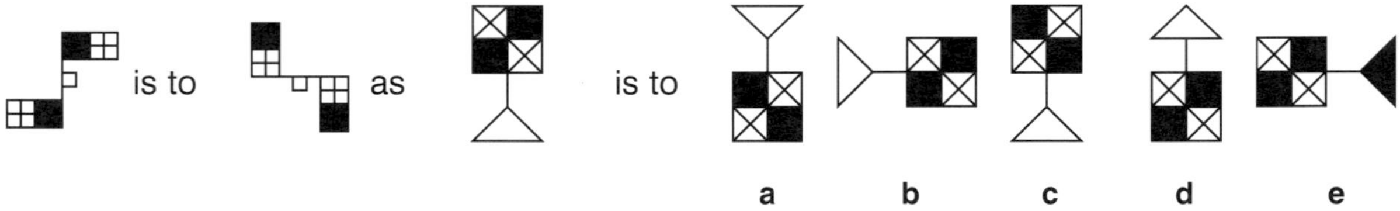

17

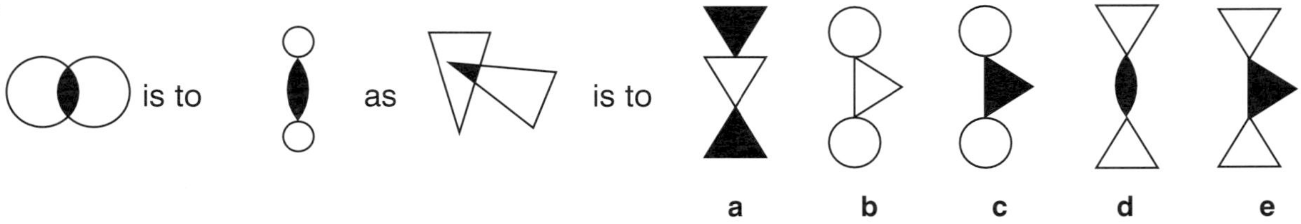

18

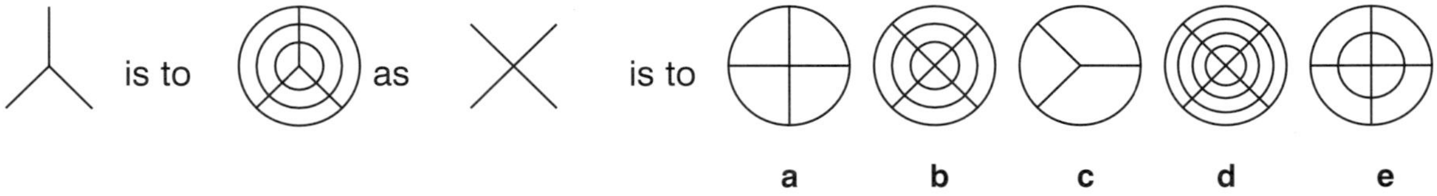

19 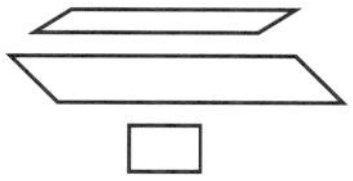 is to 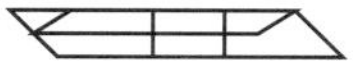 as 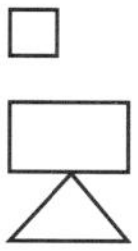 is to

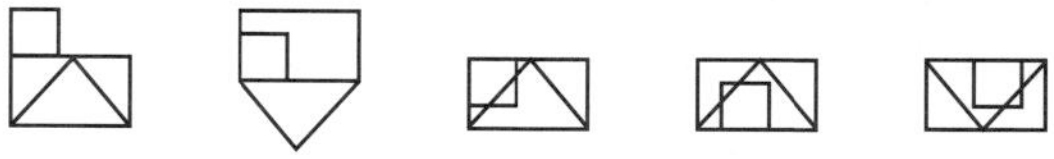

a **b** **c** **d** **e**

20  is to  as 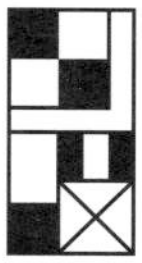 is to

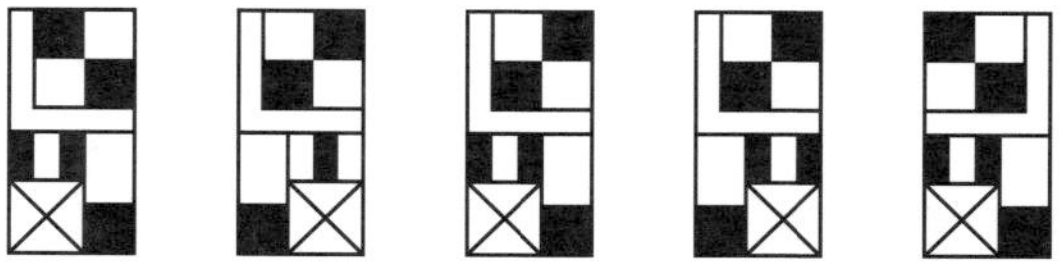

a **b** **c** **d** **e**

21 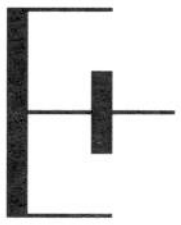 is to 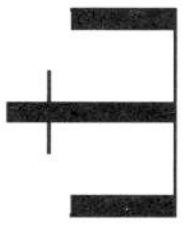 as  is to

a **b** **c** **d** **e**

22  is to 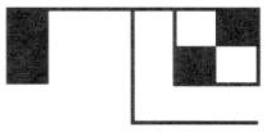 as 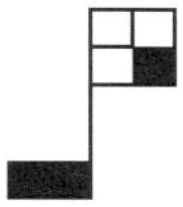 is to

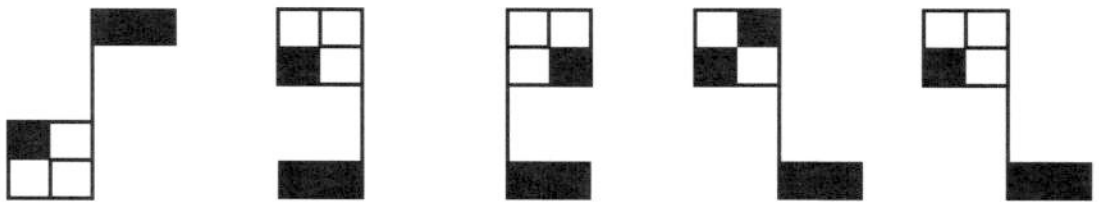

a **b** **c** **d** **e**

23  is to 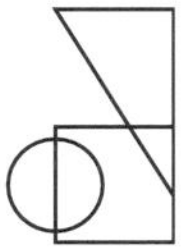 as 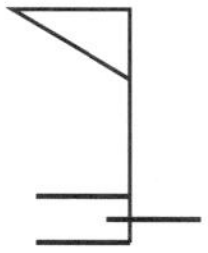 is to

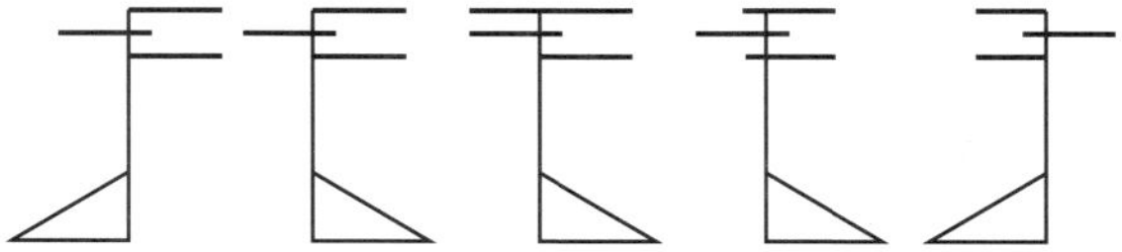

a **b** **c** **d** **e**

24 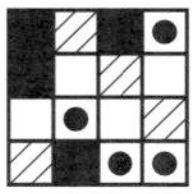 is to 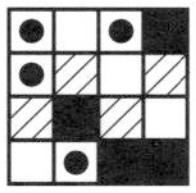 as 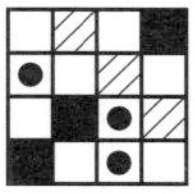 is to

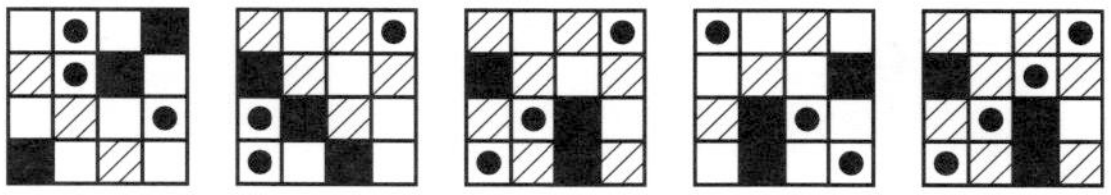

a **b** **c** **d** **e**

Look carefully at the shapes and codes given.
Select the code which matches the shape given at the end of each line.

Example

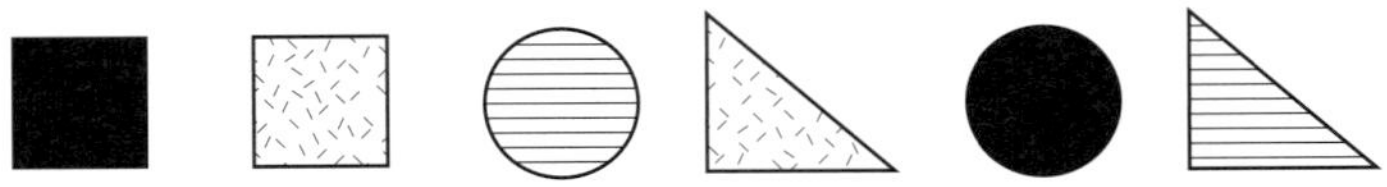

AX AY BZ CY BX ?

AY	AX	CZ	BZ	BY
a	b	(c)	d	e

25

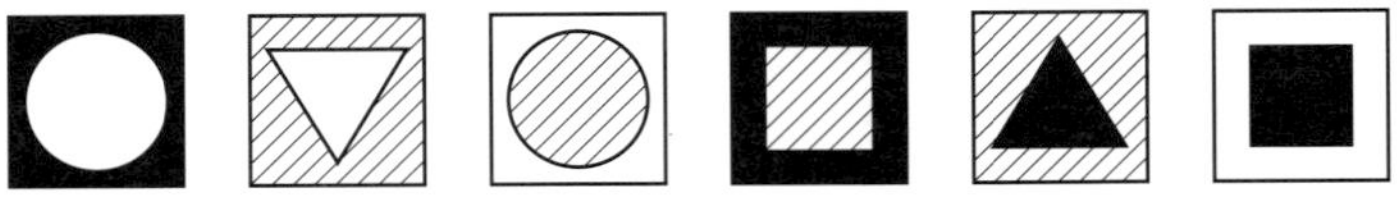

AC AB BA BC CB ?

CA	AB	AC	BA	BC
a	b	c	d	e

26

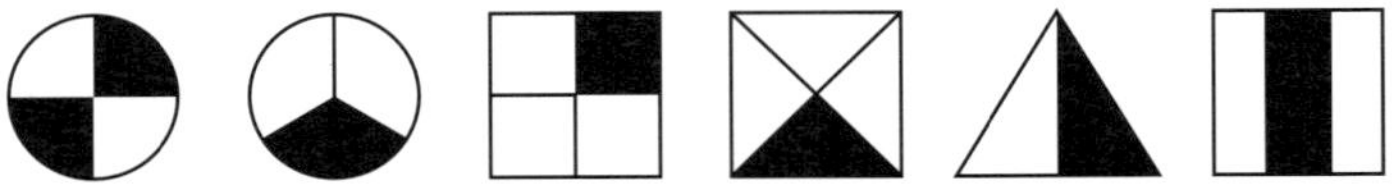

XA YA ZB ZB XC ?

YB	ZB	YC	XA	YA
a	b	c	d	e

27

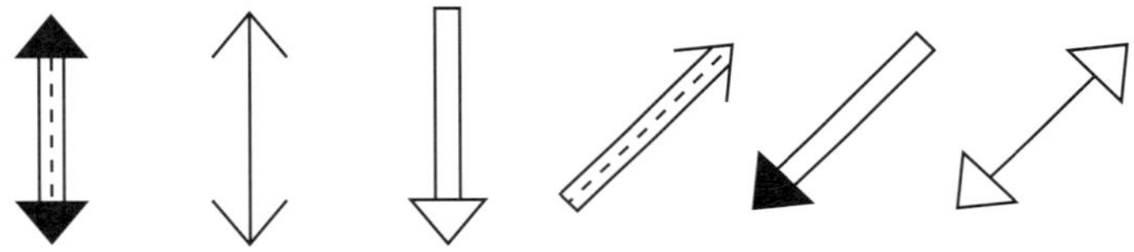

SM TN UO TM SO ?

SM	SN	UO	TN	UN
a	b	c	d	e

28

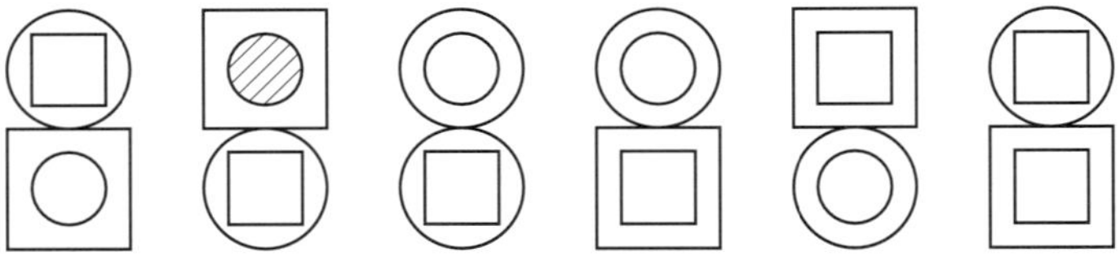

DF FD ED EG GE ?

DG	FD	FG	DE	GG
a	b	c	d	e

29

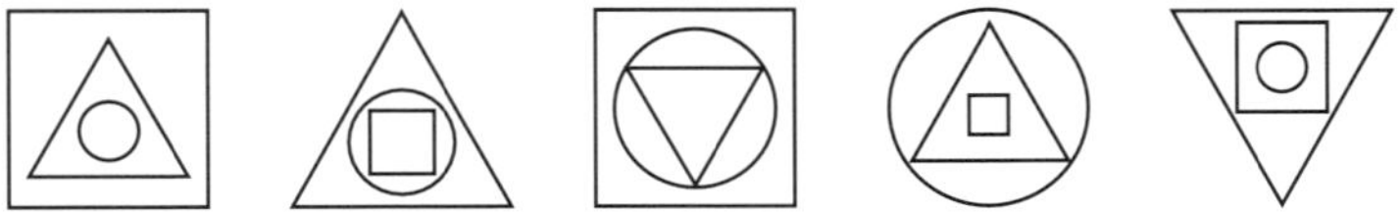

RX SY RZ TY ?

SZ	SX	RY	TZ	TR
a	b	c	d	e

30

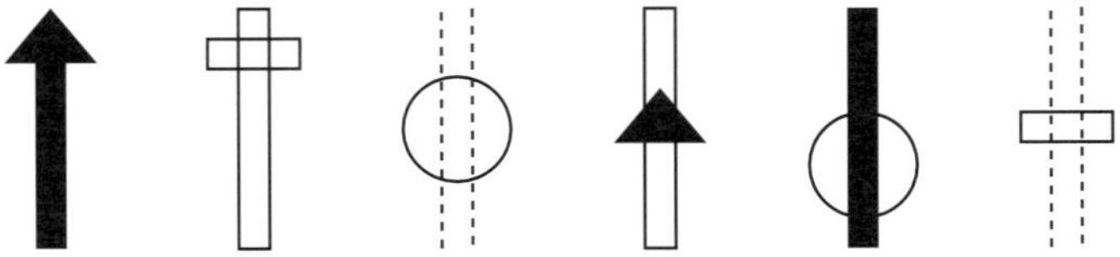

HC JB KA JC HA ?

KC	HB	JA	KB	HA
a	b	c	d	e

Which shape is most similar to the shapes in the group on the left? Circle the letter.

Example

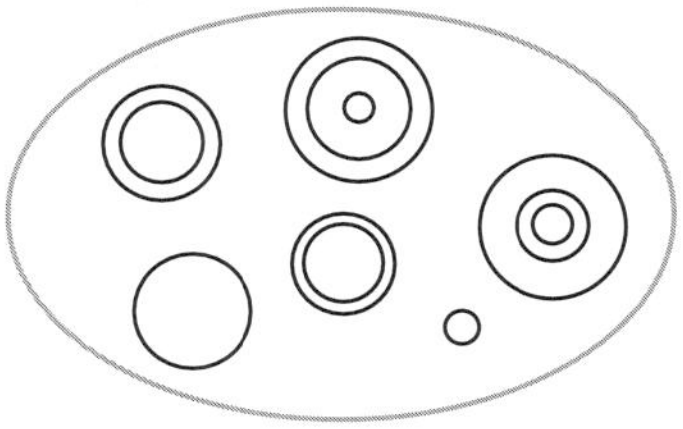

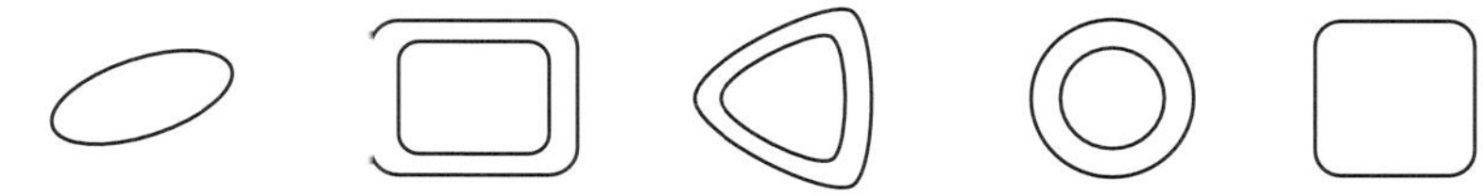

a b c d e

31

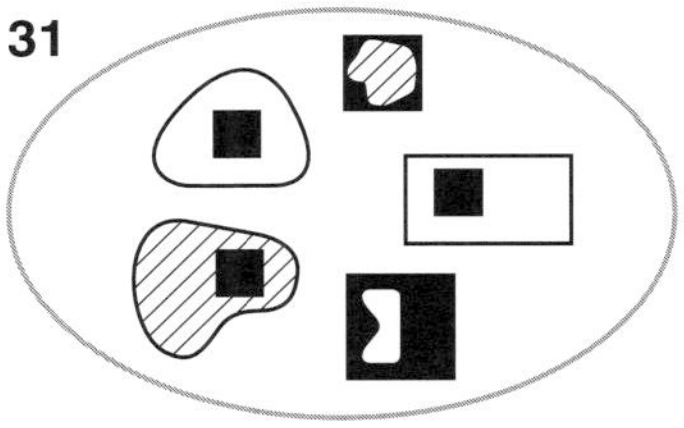

a b c d e

32

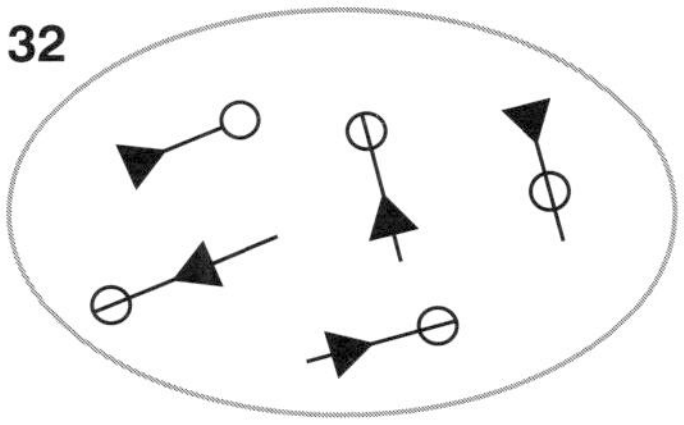

a b c d e

33

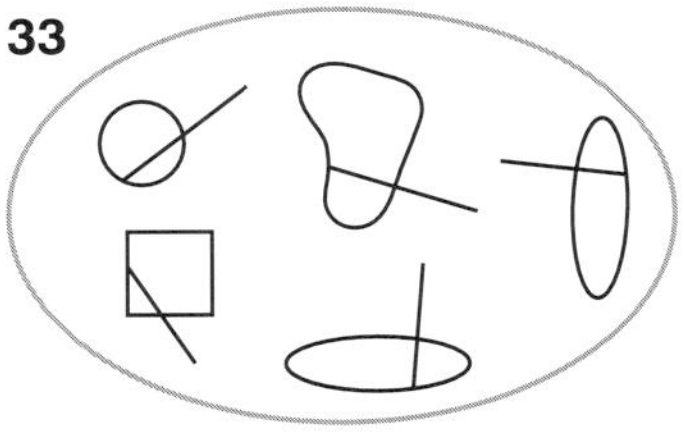

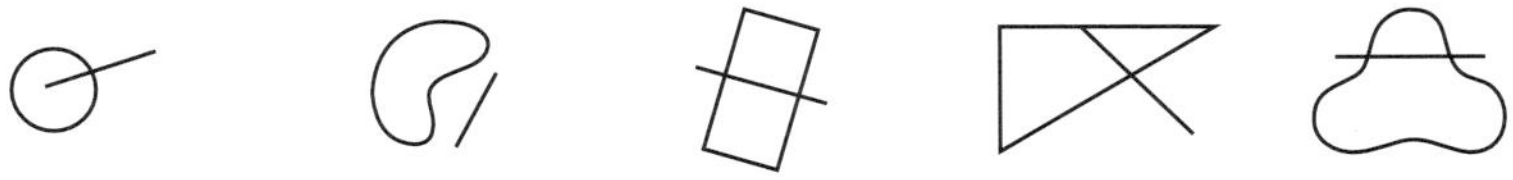

a b c d e

34

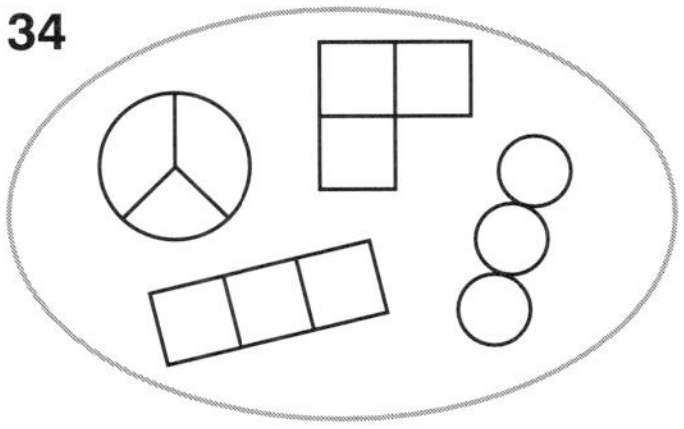

a b c d e

35

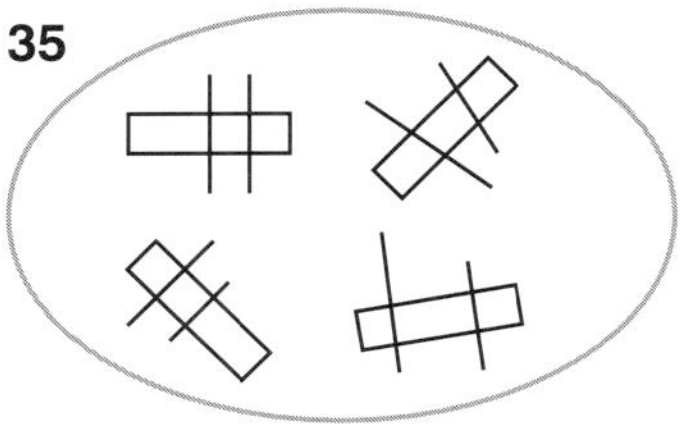

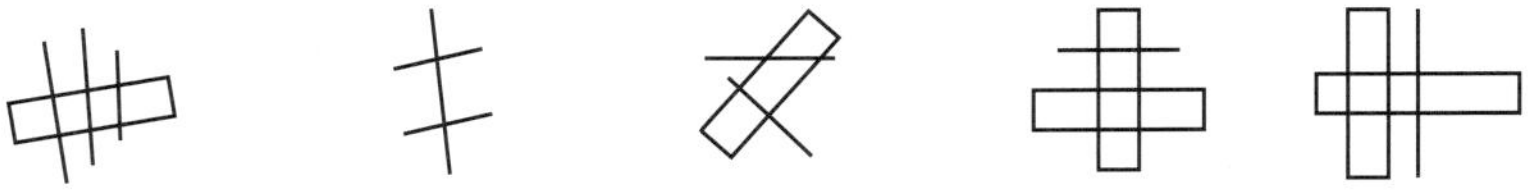

a b c d e

36

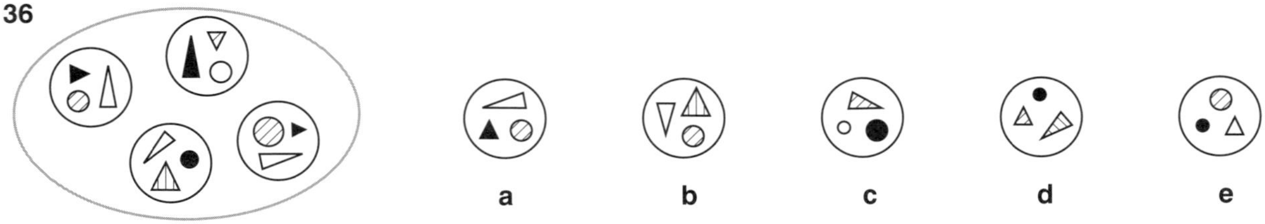

37

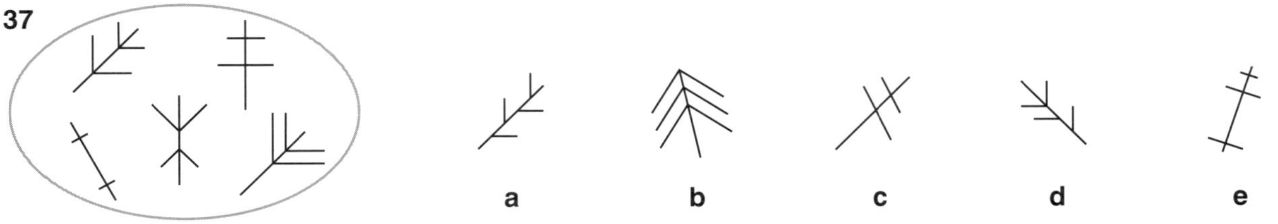

38

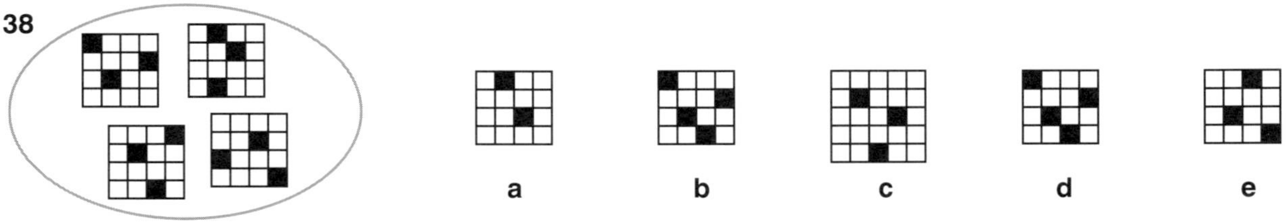

39

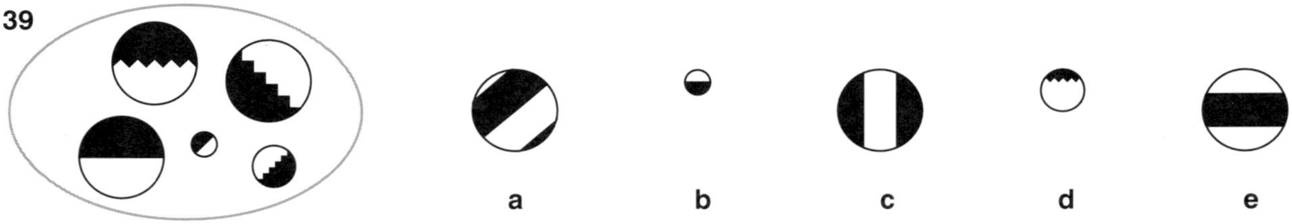

40

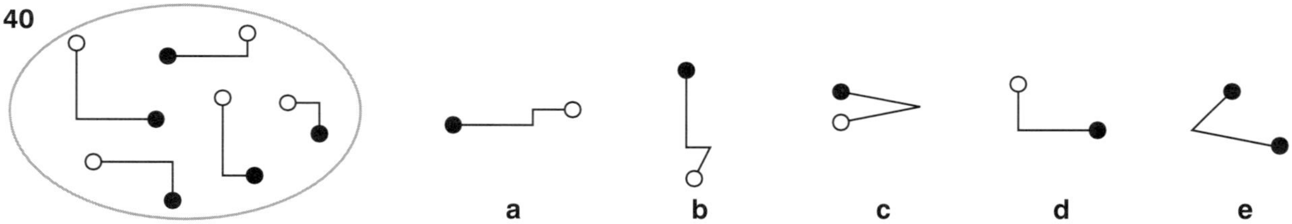

41

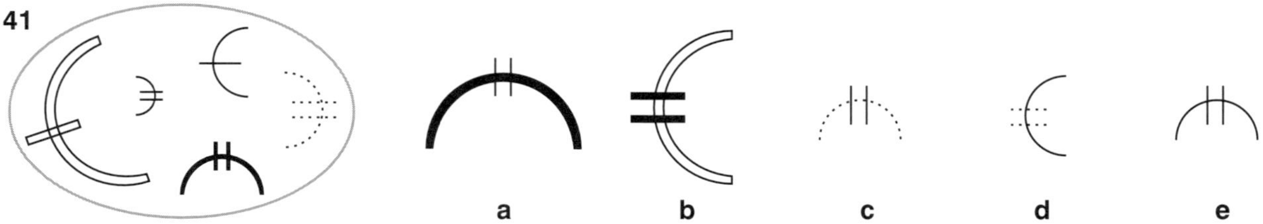

42

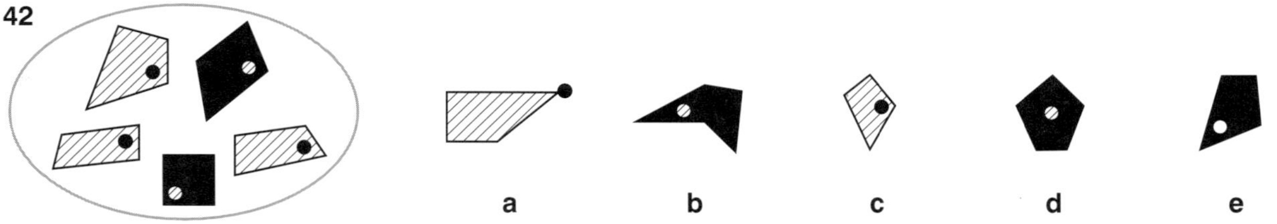

Find the shape or pattern which completes the square. Circle the letter.

Example

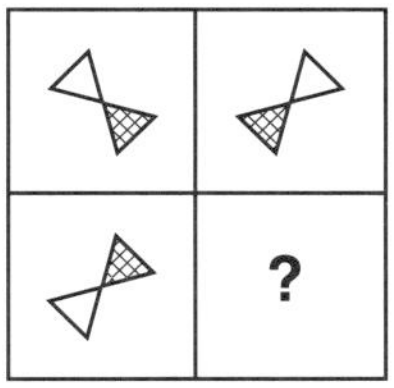

a b c d e

43

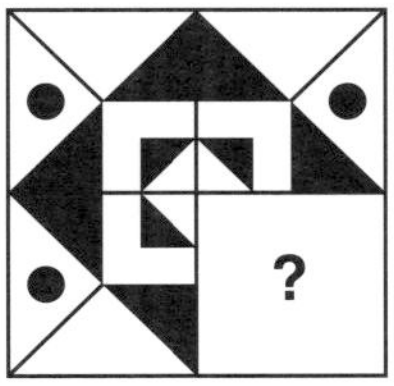

a b c d e

44

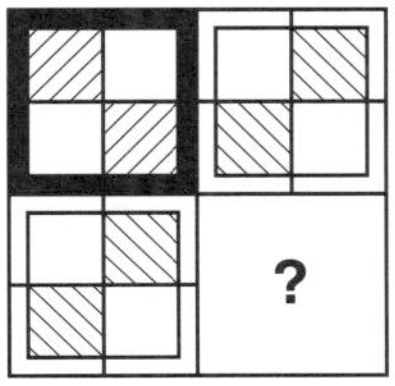

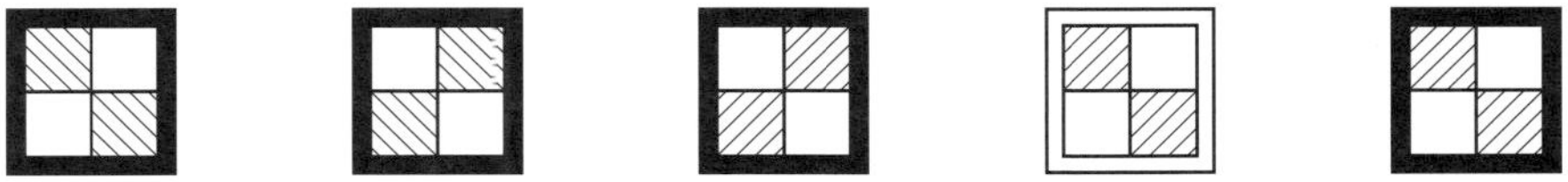

a b c d e

45

a b c d e

46

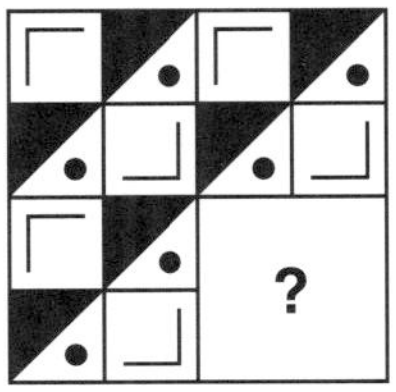

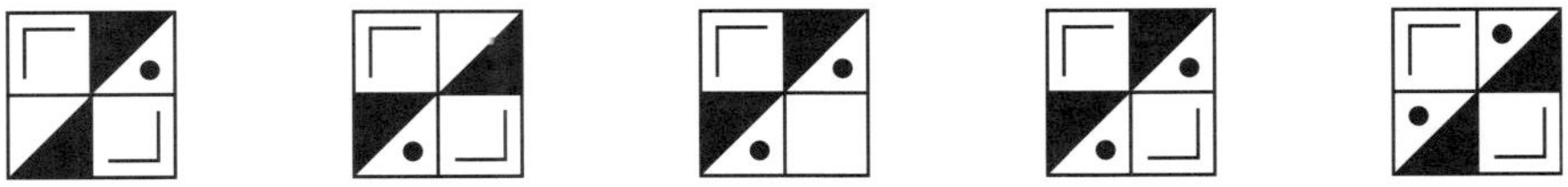

a b c d e

47

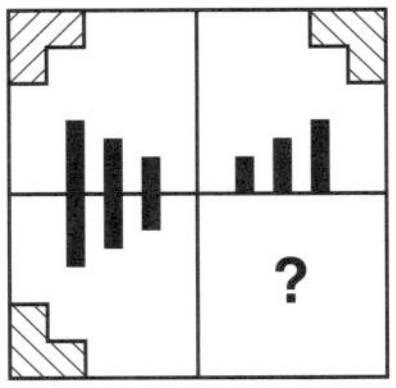

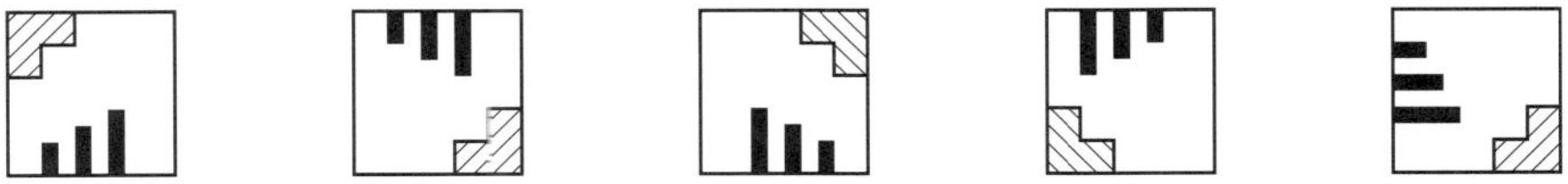

a b c d e

48

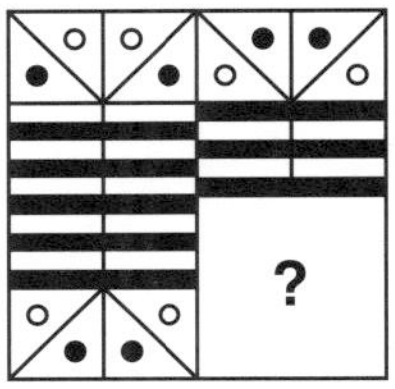

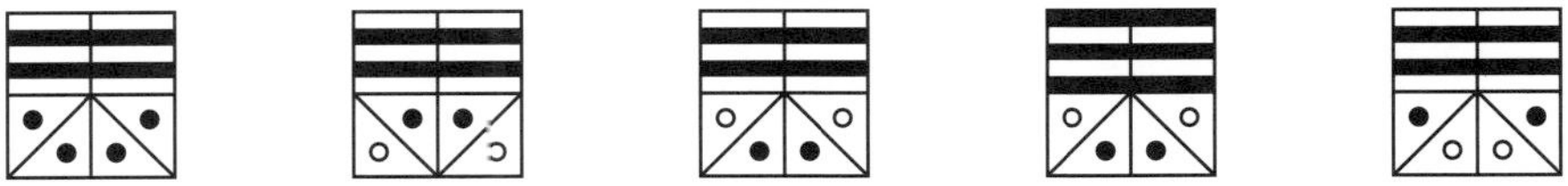

a b c d e

49

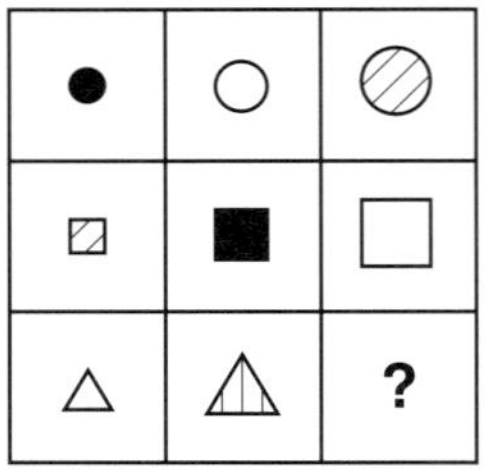

a b c d e

50

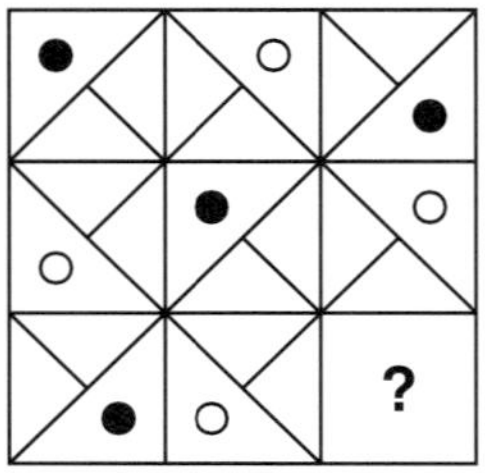

a b c d e

51

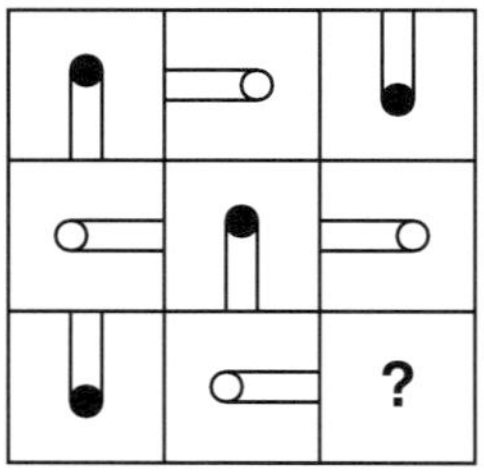

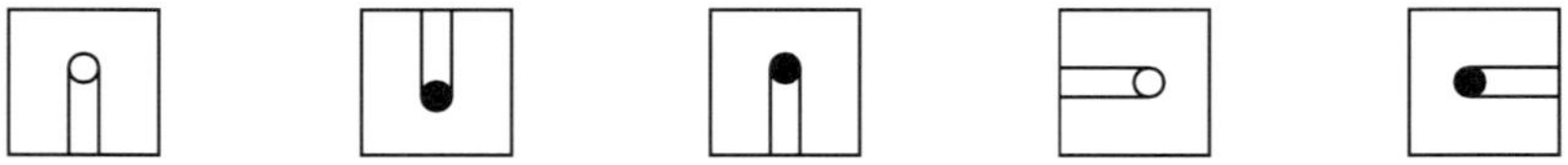

a b c d e

52

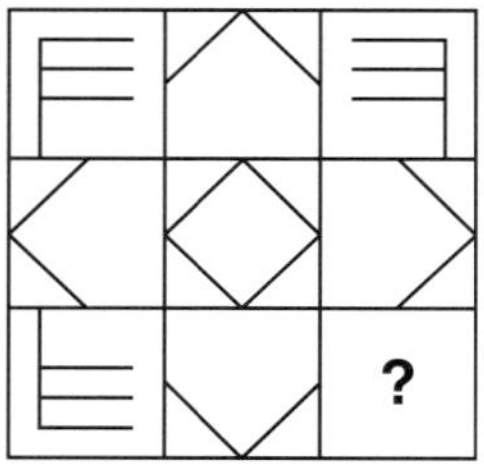

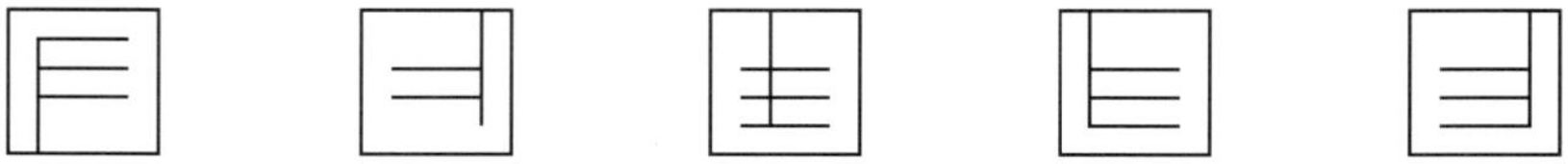

a b c d e

53

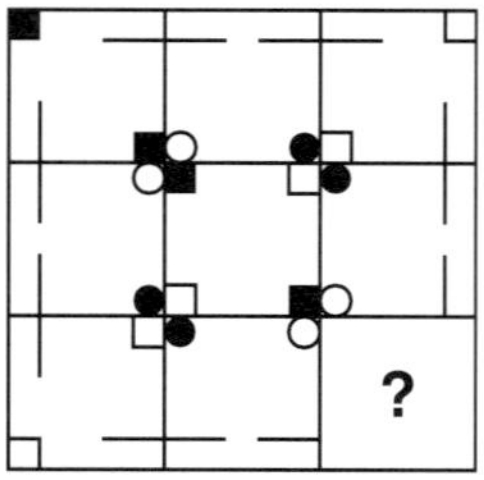

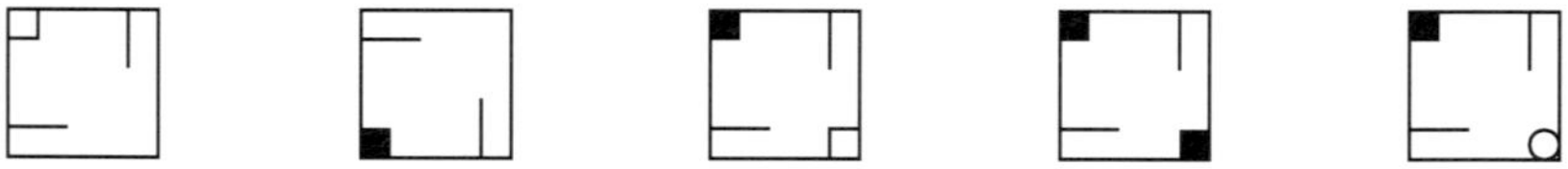

a b c d e

54

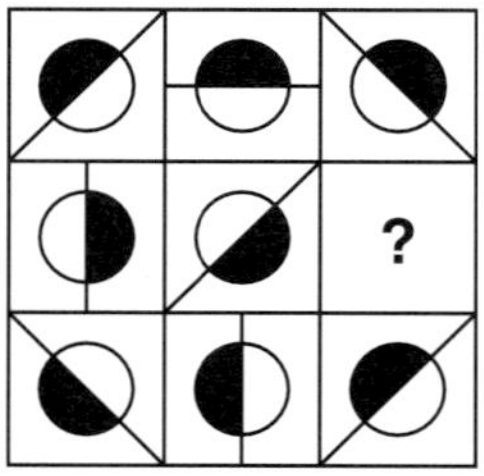

a b c d e

In which larger shape or pattern is the smaller shape hidden? Circle the letter.

Example

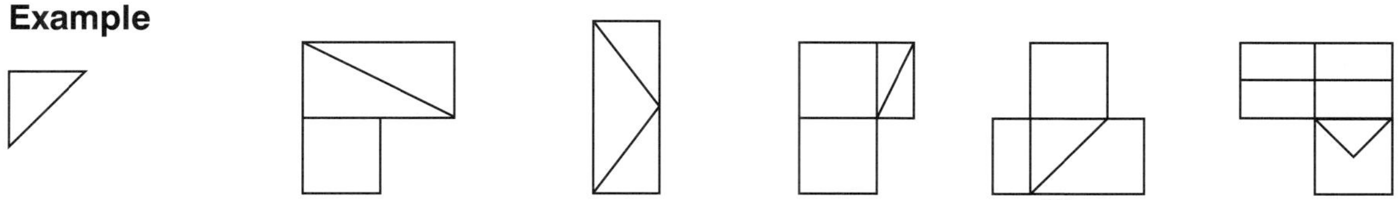

a b c d e

55 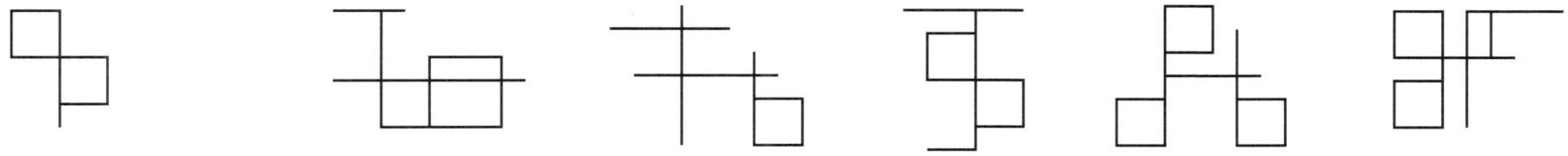

a b c d e

56 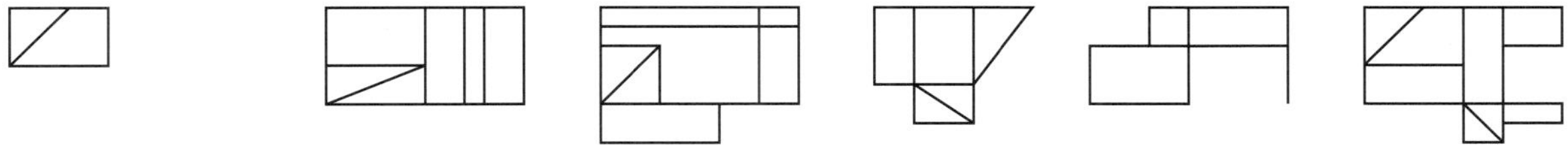

a b c d e

57 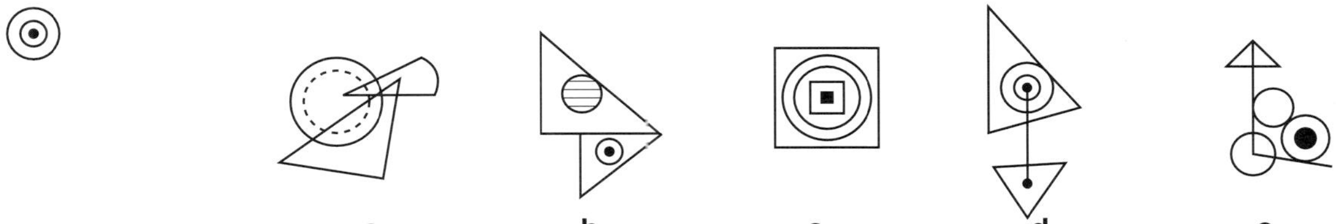

a b c d e

58 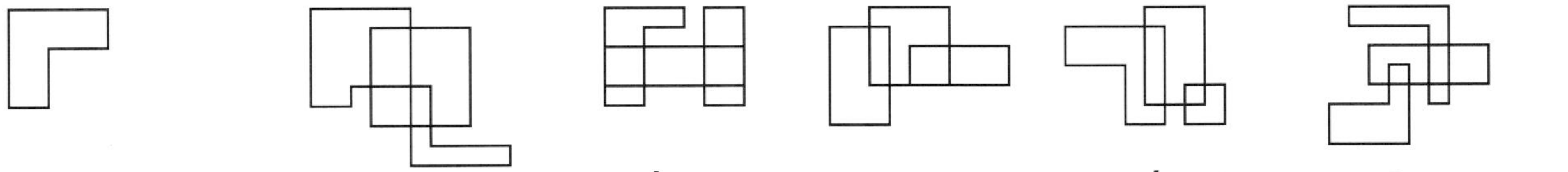

a b c d e

59 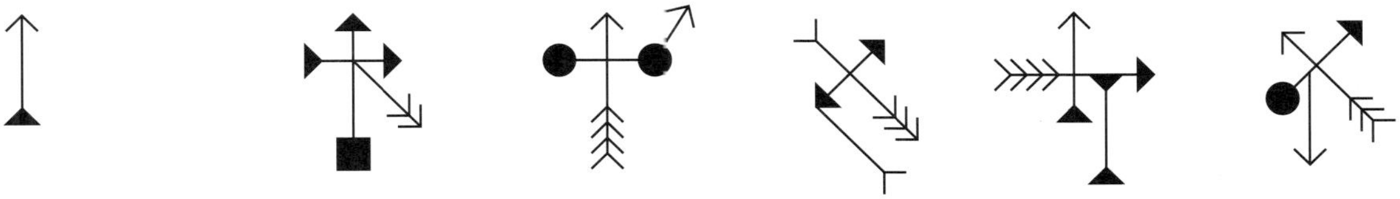

a b c d e

60 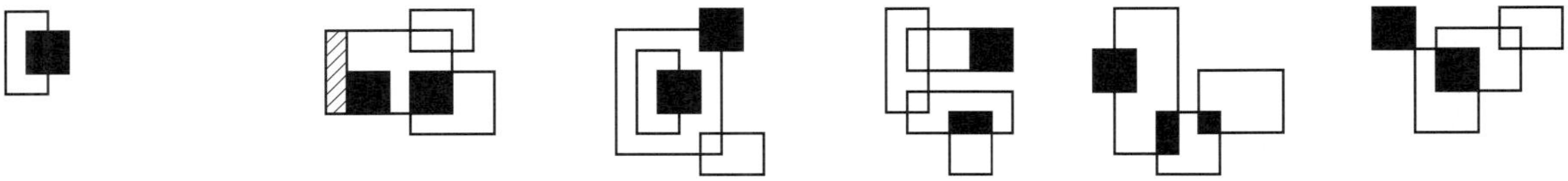

a b c d e

Paper 6

Find the shape or pattern which completes or continues the given series. Circle the letter.

Example

1
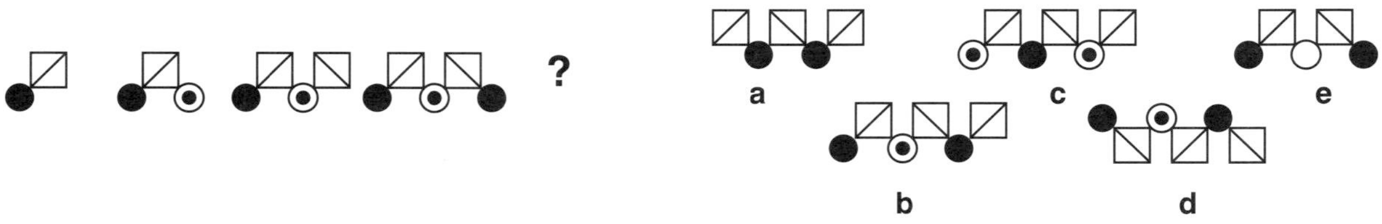

2
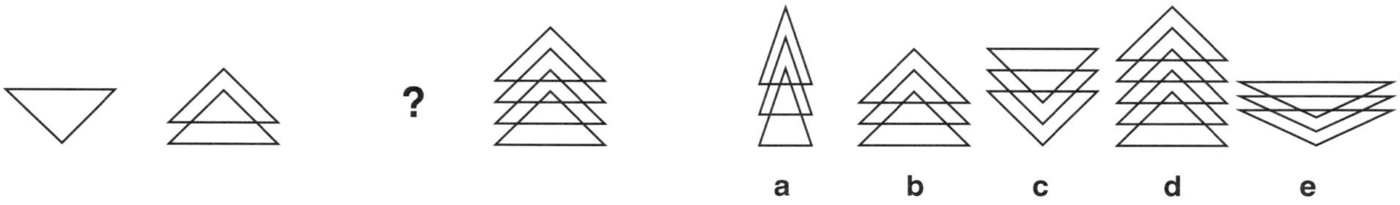

3
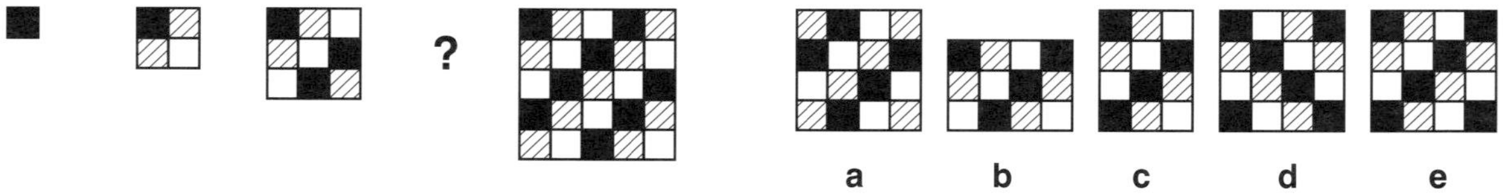

4

5
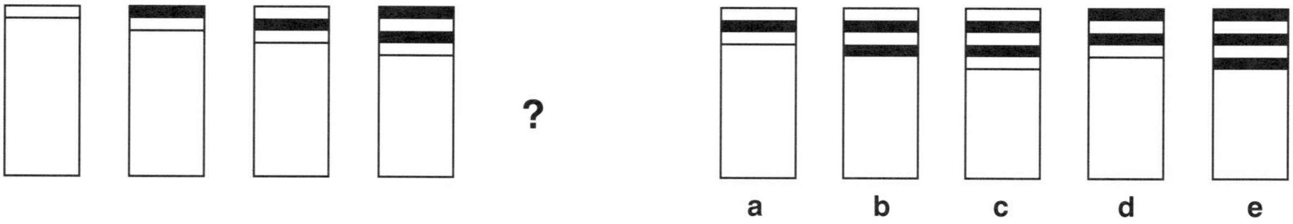

6

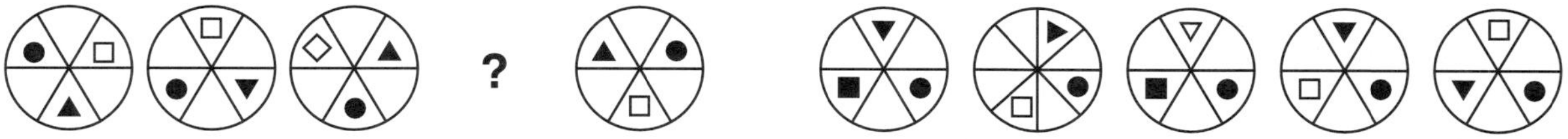

a b c d e

7

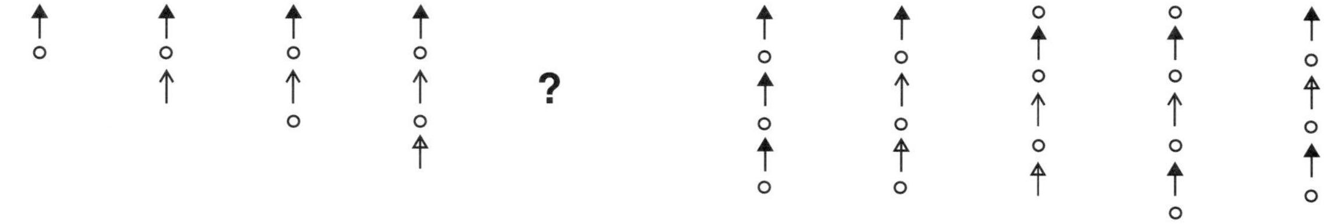

a b c d e

8

a b c d e

9

a b c d e

10

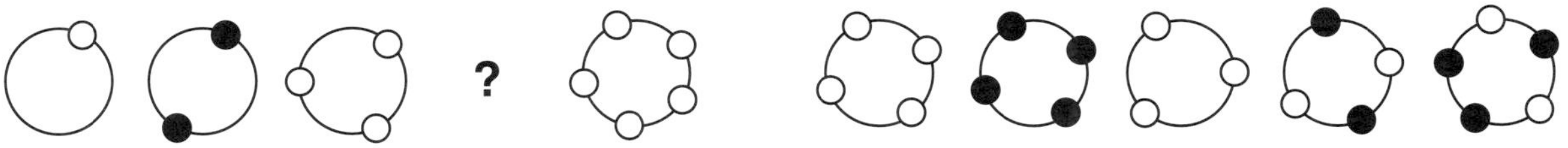

a b c d e

11

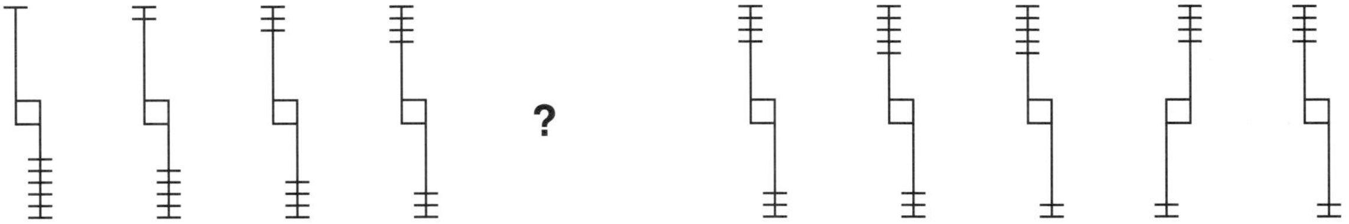

a b c d e

12

a b c d e

Which shape or pattern is most similar to the ones in the group on the left? Circle the letter.

Example

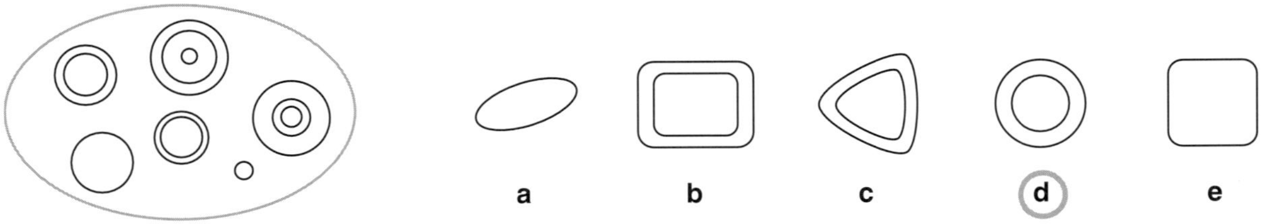

13

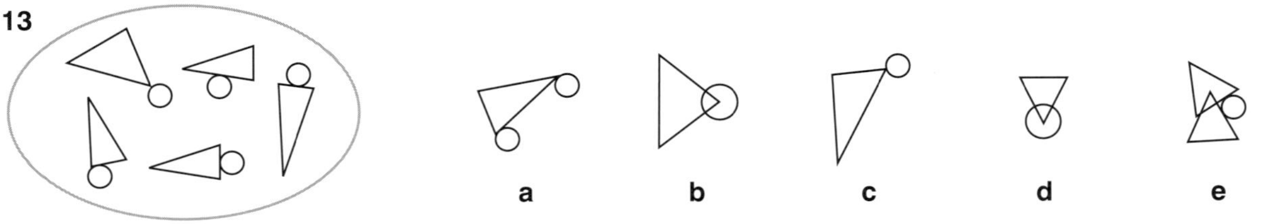

14

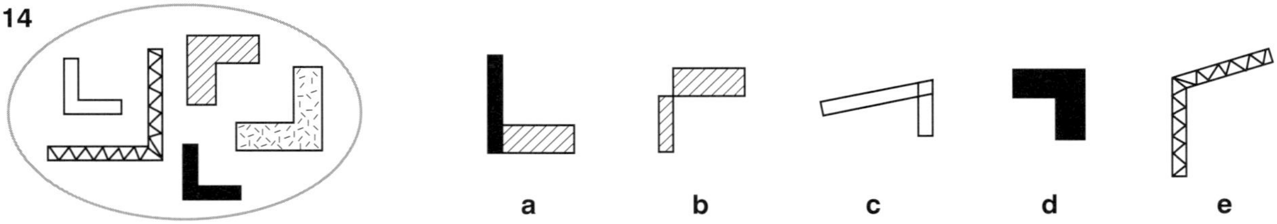

15

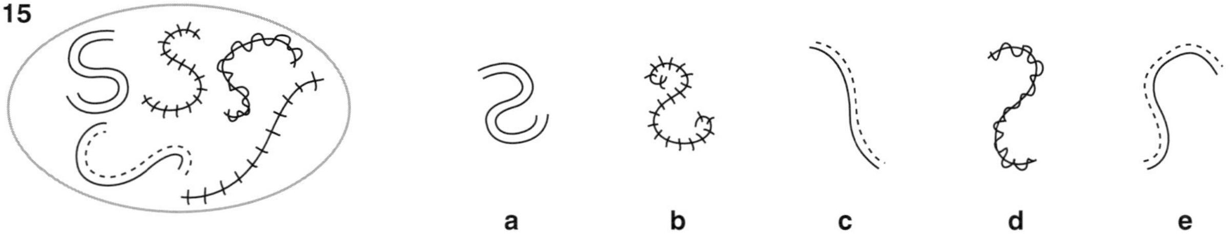

16

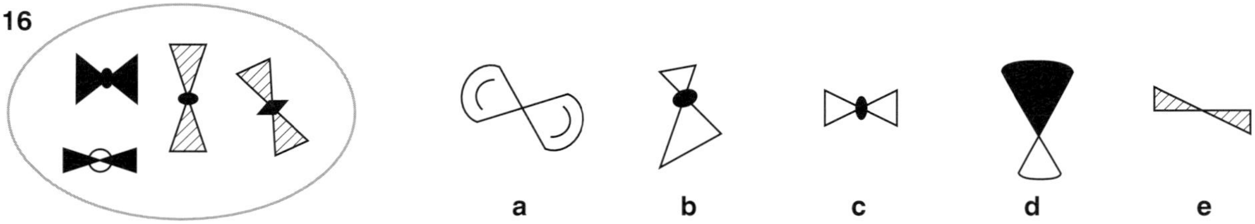

17

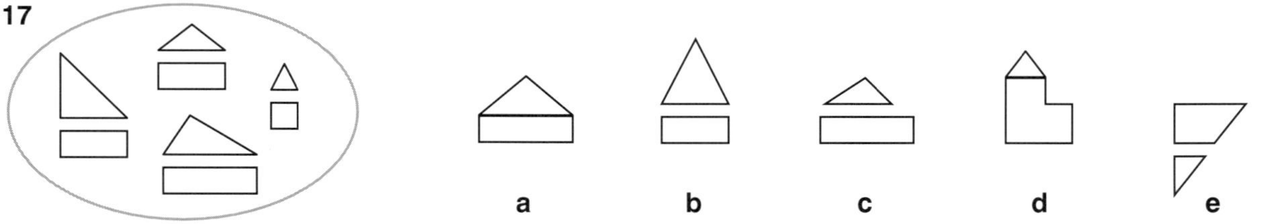

18

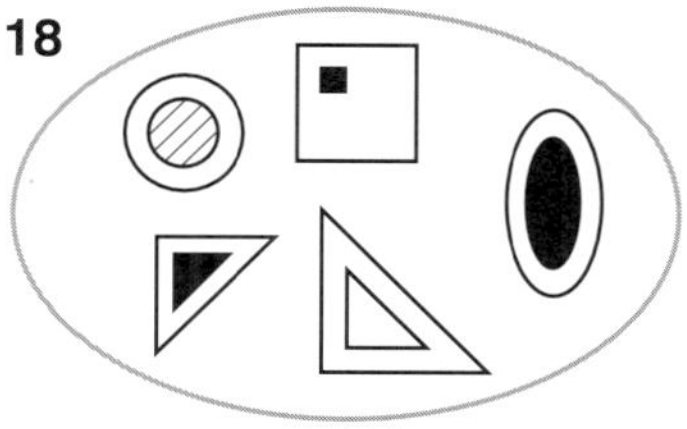

a b c d e

19

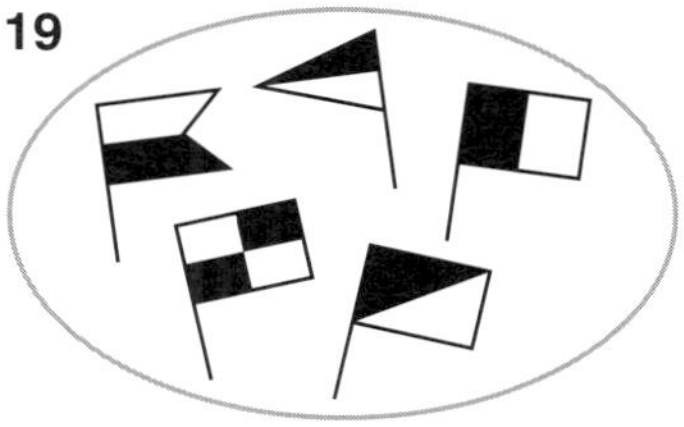

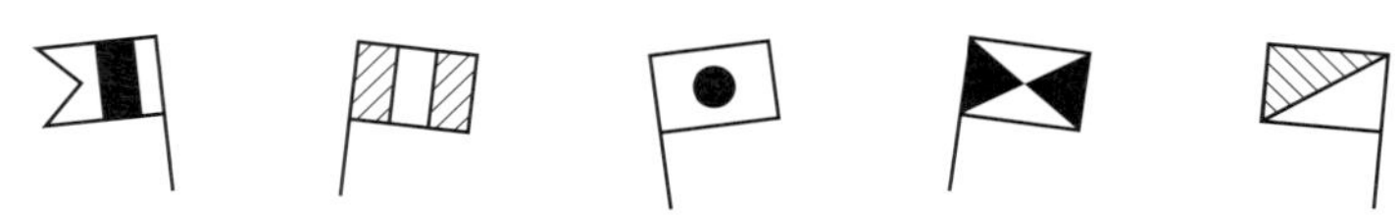

a b c d e

20

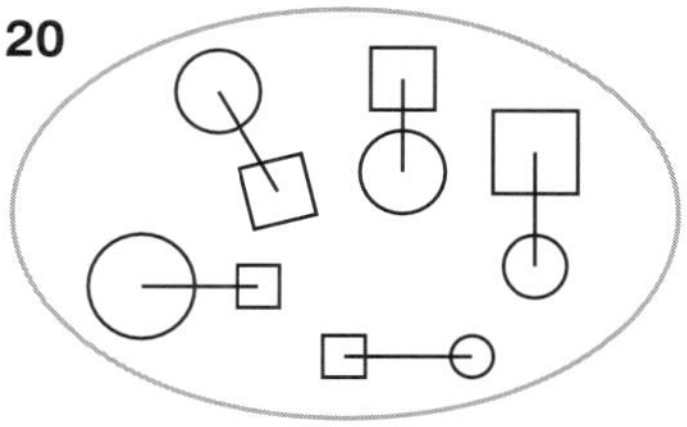

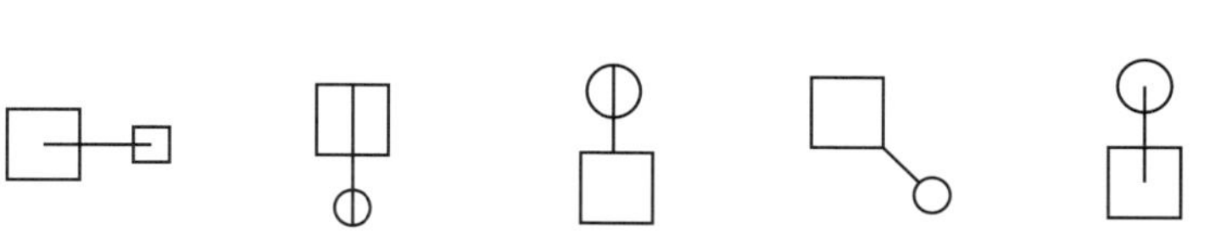

a b c d e

21

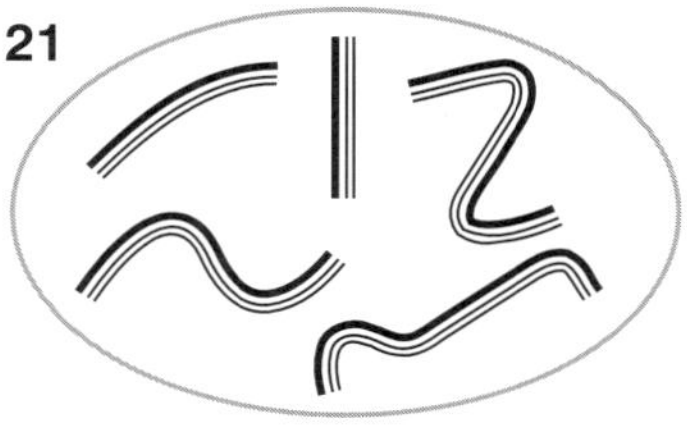

a b c d e

22

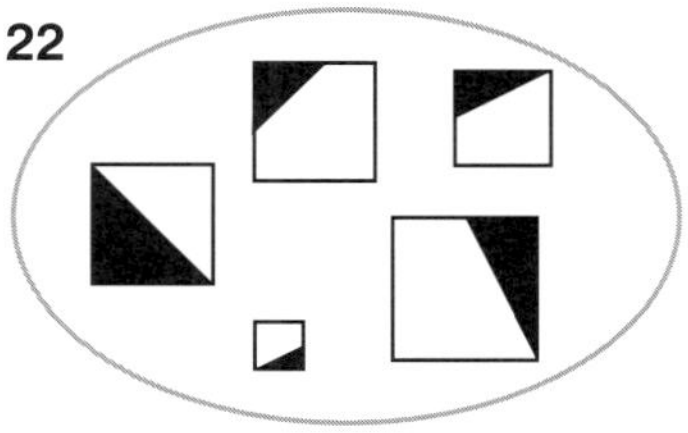

a b c d e

23

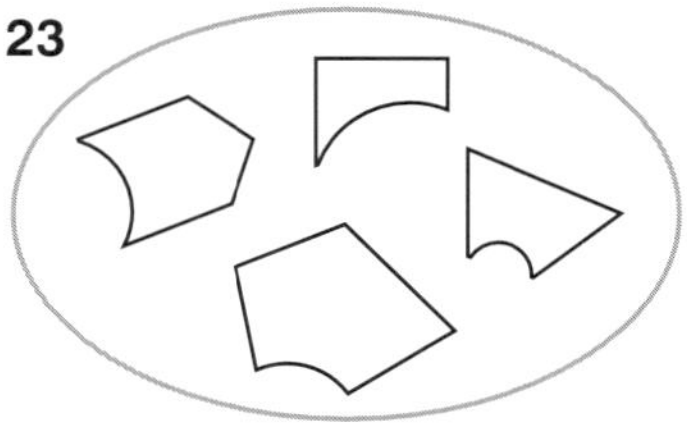

a b c d e

24

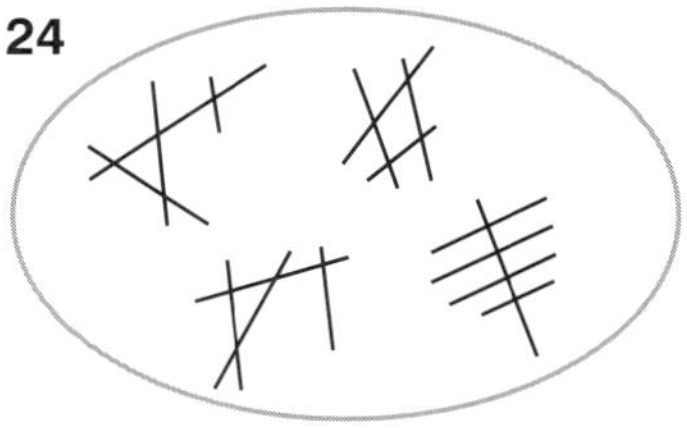

a b c d e

Which shape on the right is the reflection of the shape given on the left? Circle the letter.

Example

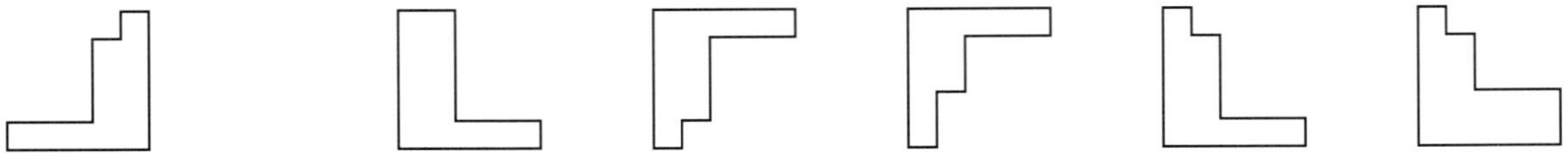

a b c d e

25

a b c d e

26

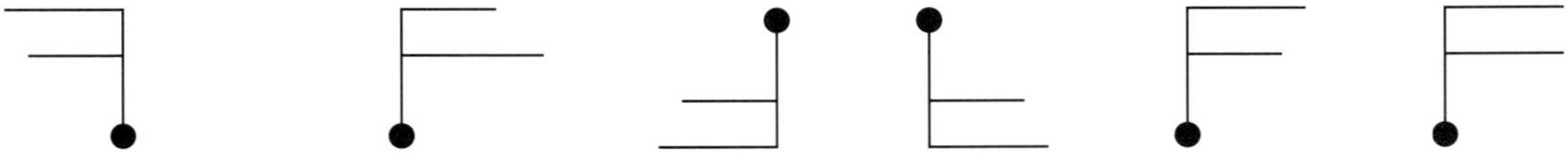

a b c d e

27

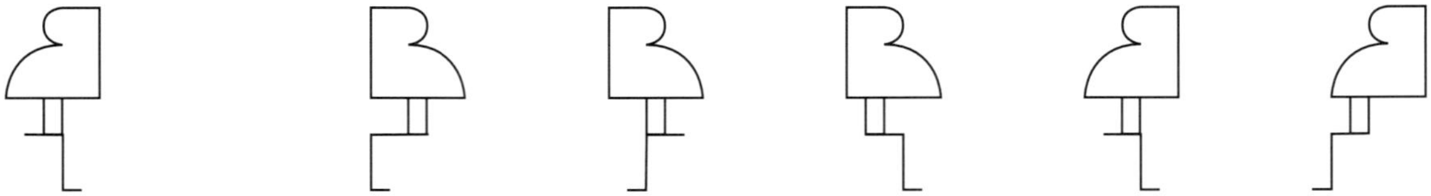

a b c d e

28

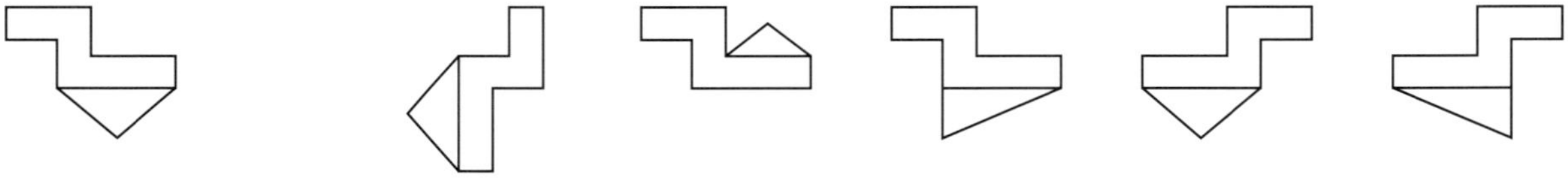

a b c d e

29

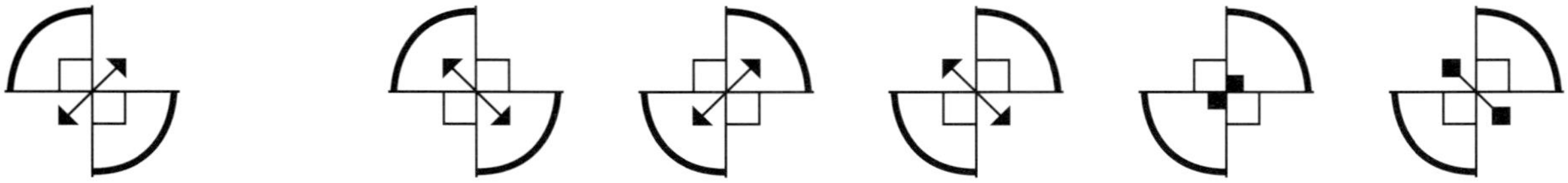

a b c d e

30

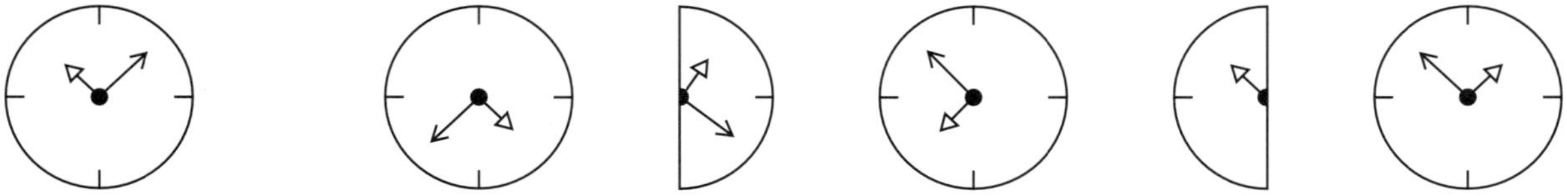

a b c d e

Find the shape or pattern which completes the second pair in the same way as the first pair. Circle the letter.

Example

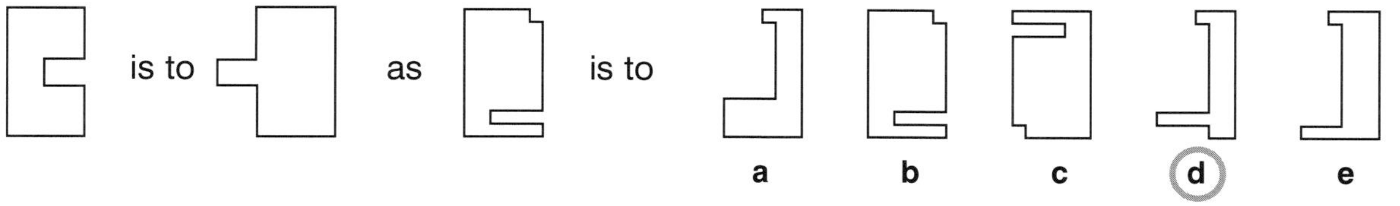

31

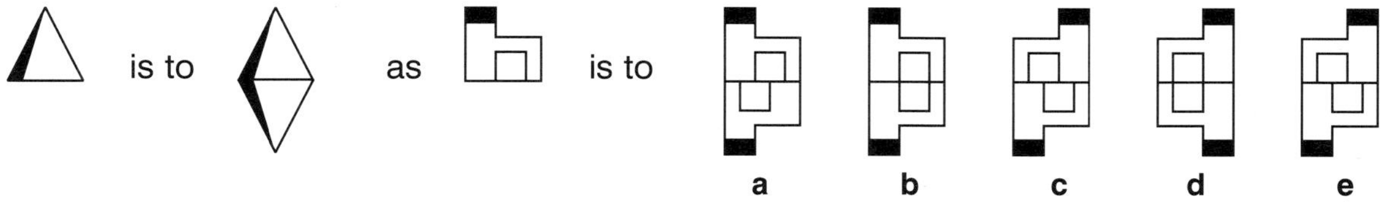

32

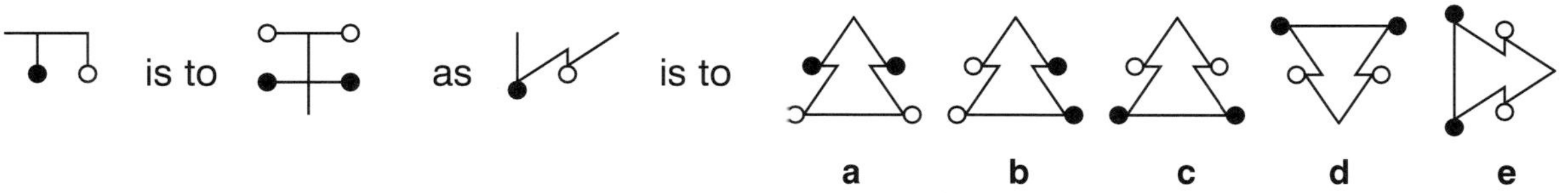

33

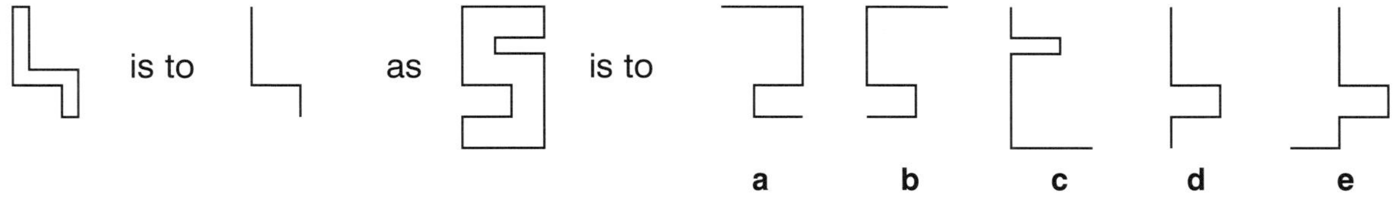

34

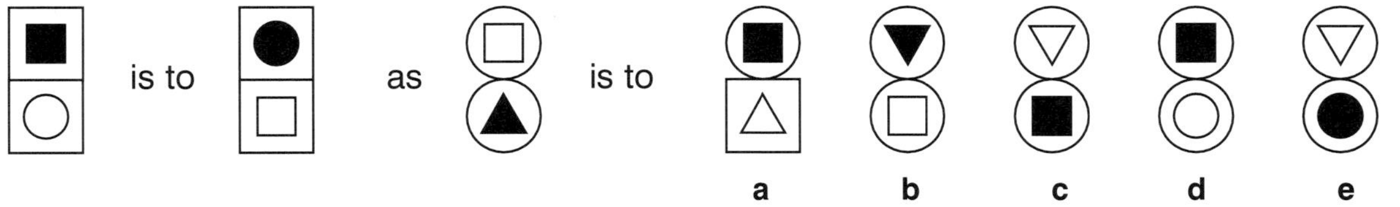

35

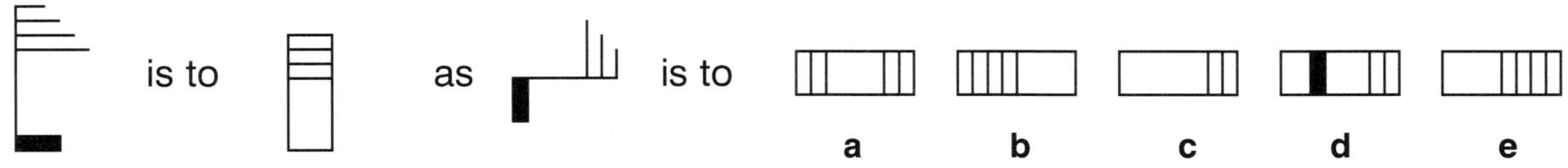

36

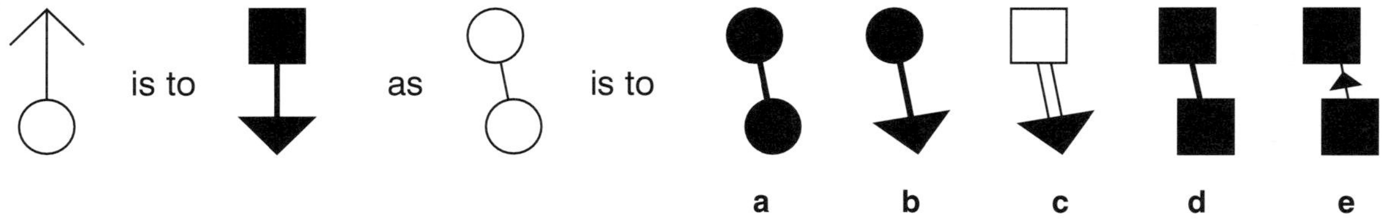

37  is to  as 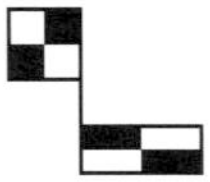 is to

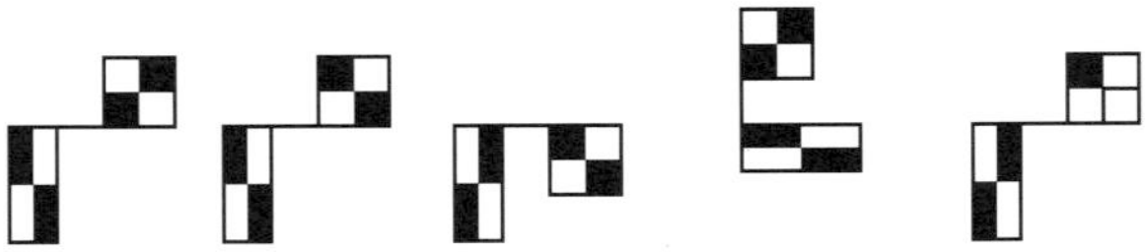

a b c d e

38  is to  as 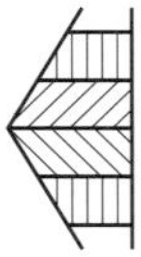 is to

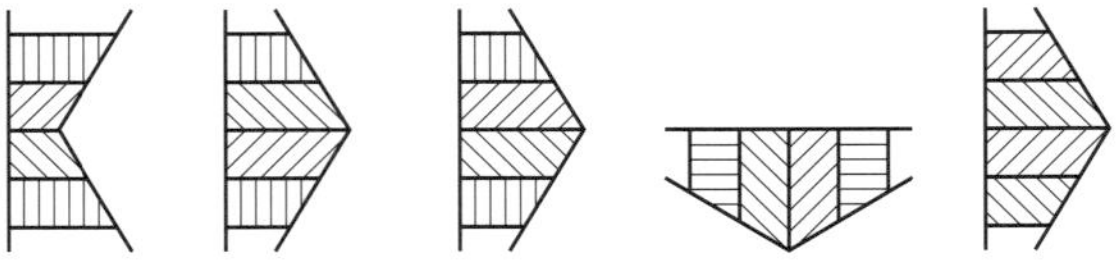

a b c d e

39 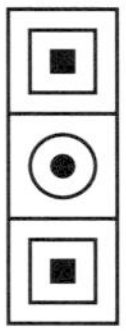 is to 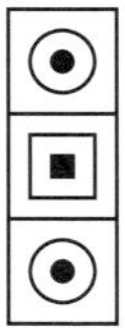 as 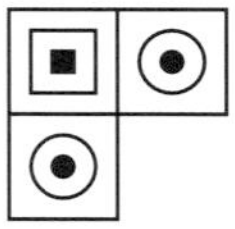 is to

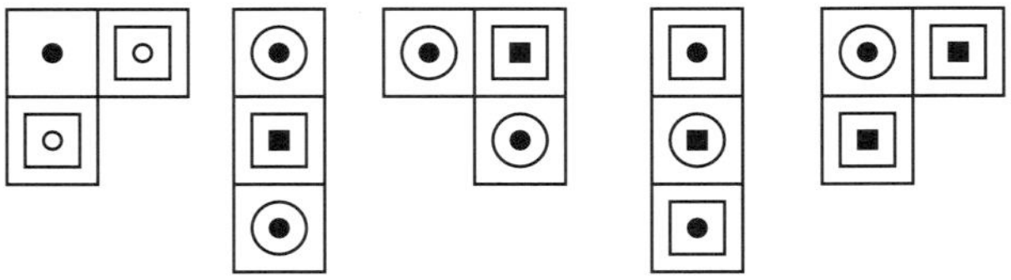

a b c d e

40 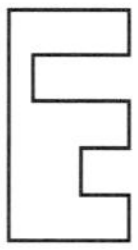 is to 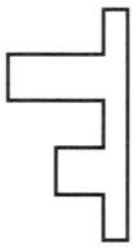 as 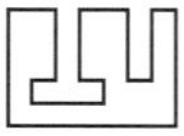 is to

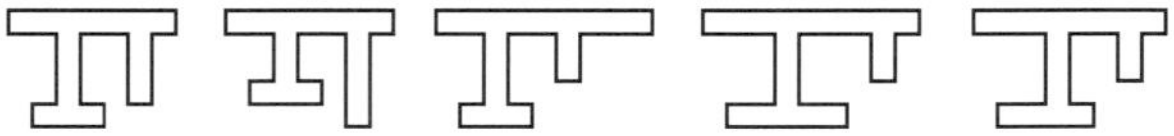

a b c d e

41  is to  as 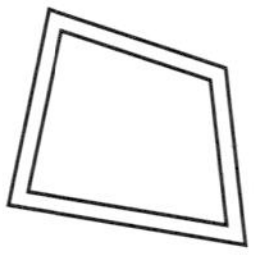 is to

a b c d e

42 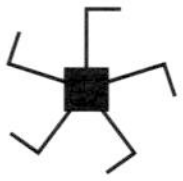 is to 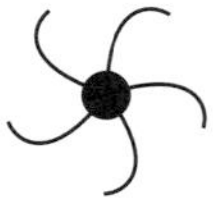 as  is to

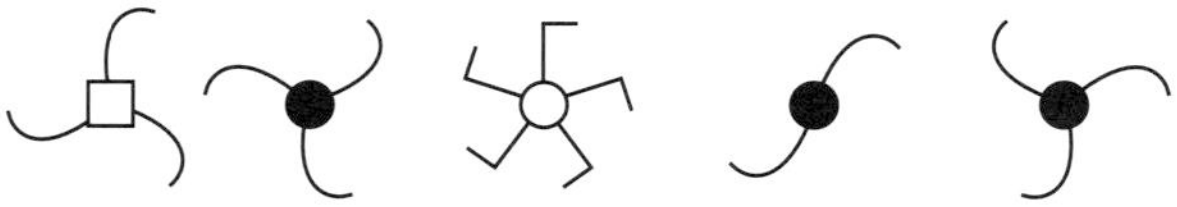

a b c d e

Which cube could not be made from the given net? Circle the letter.

Example

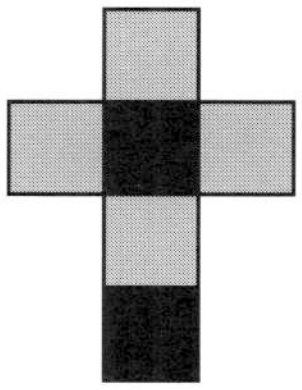

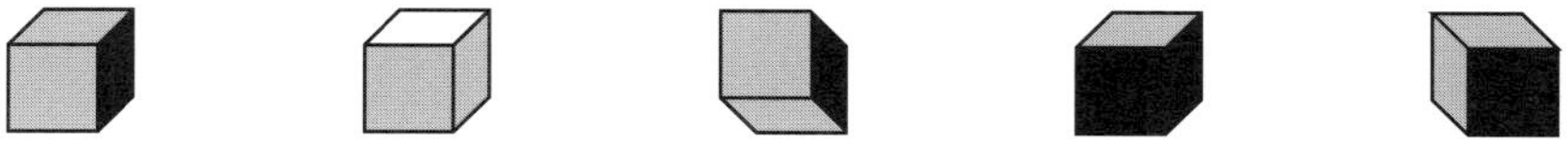

a b c d e

43

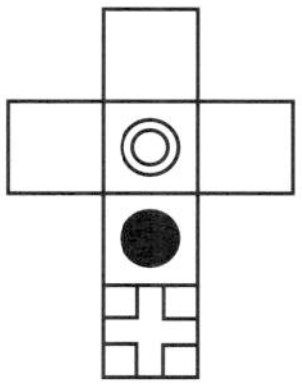

a b c d e

44

a b c d e

45

a b c d e

46

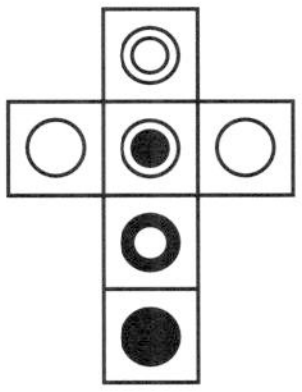

a b c d e

47

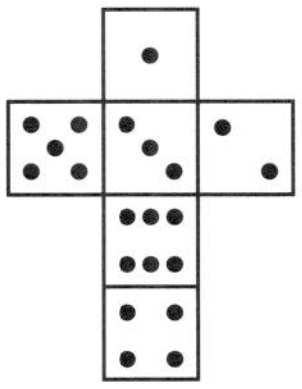

a b c d e

48

a b c d e

Find the shape or pattern which completes the square. Circle the letter.

Example

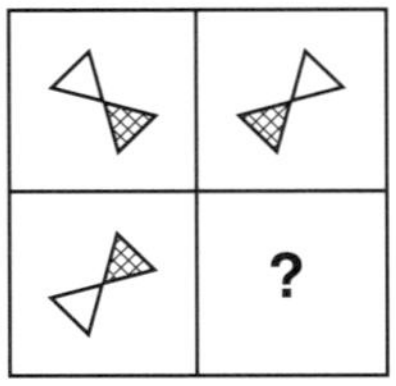

a b c d e

49

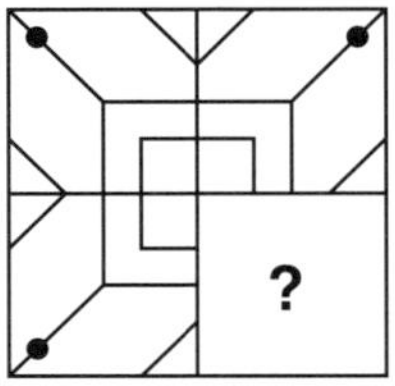

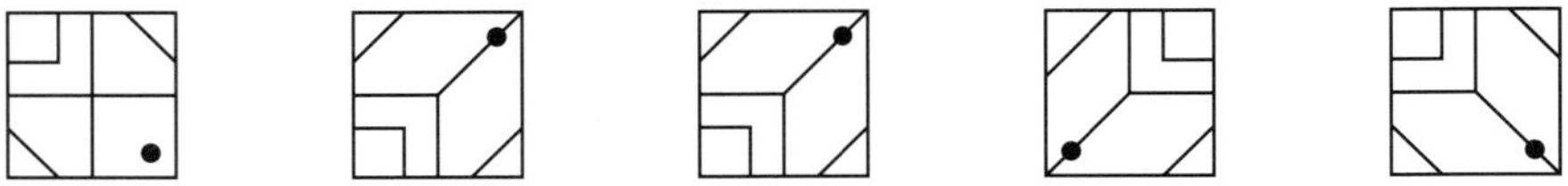

a b c d e

50

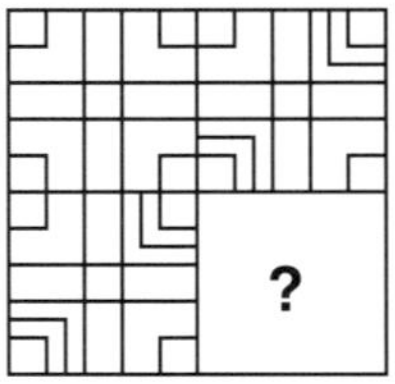

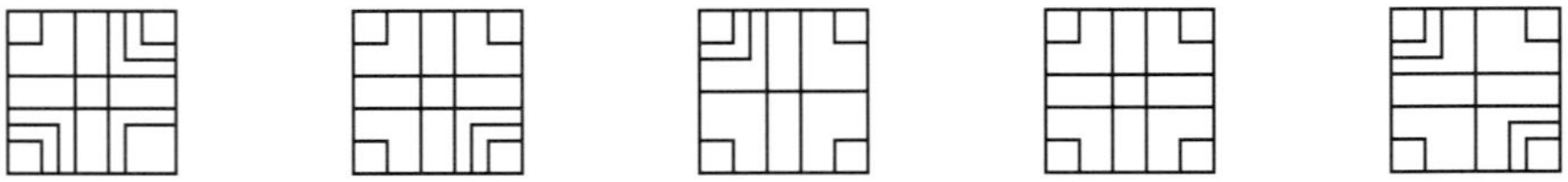

a b c d e

51

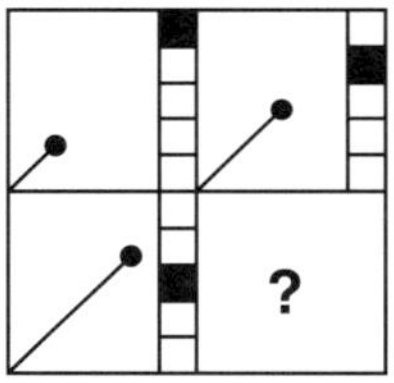

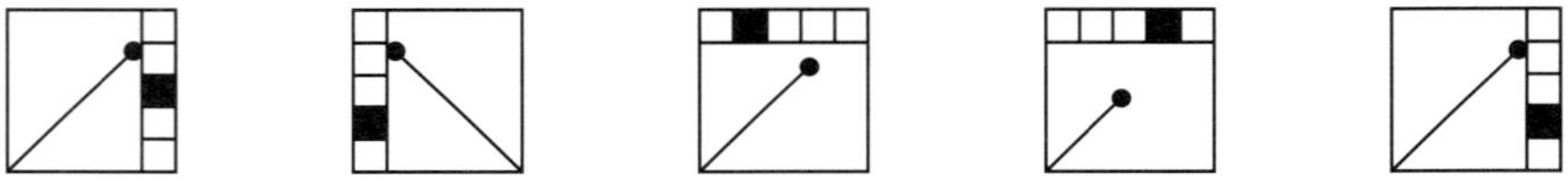

a b c d e

52

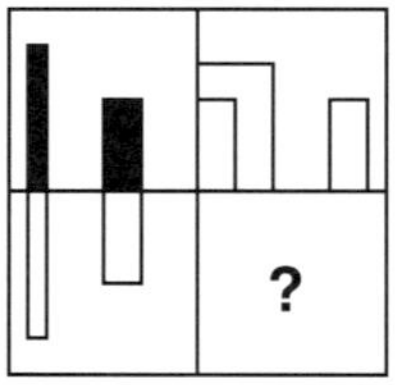

a b c d e

53

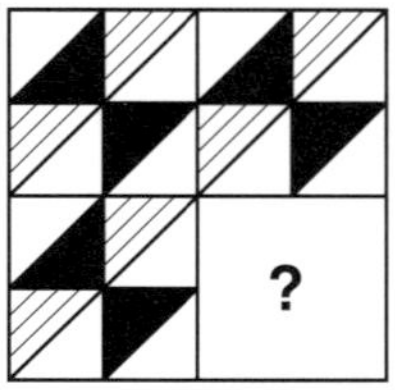

a b c d e

54

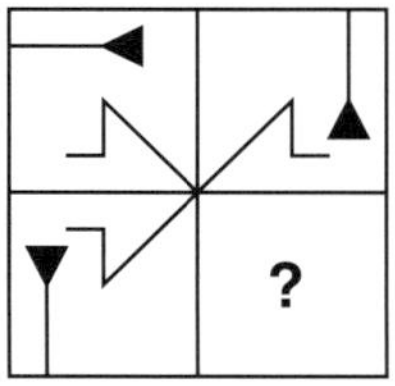

a b c d e

55

a b c d e

56

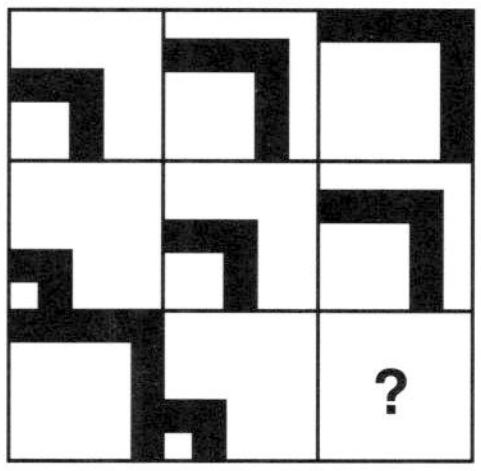

a b c d e

57

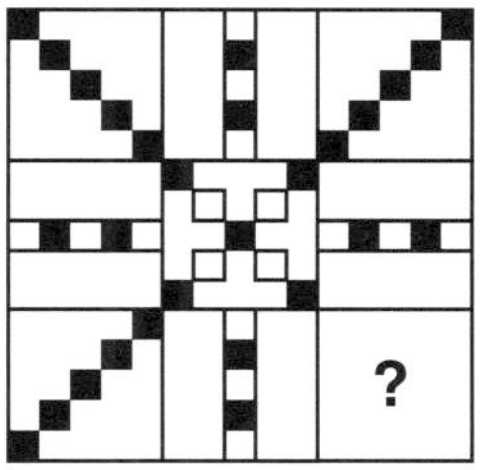

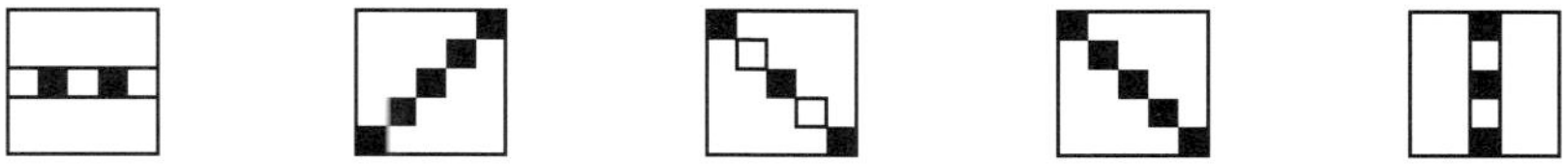

a b c d e

58

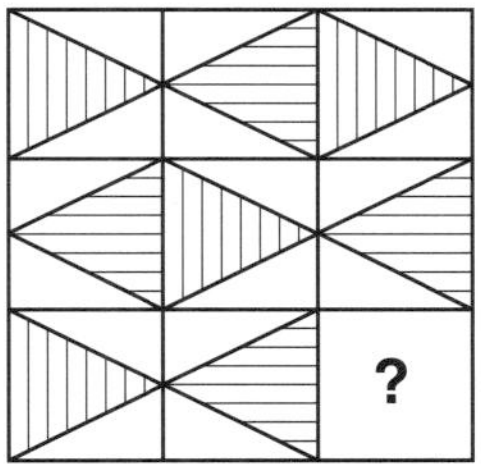

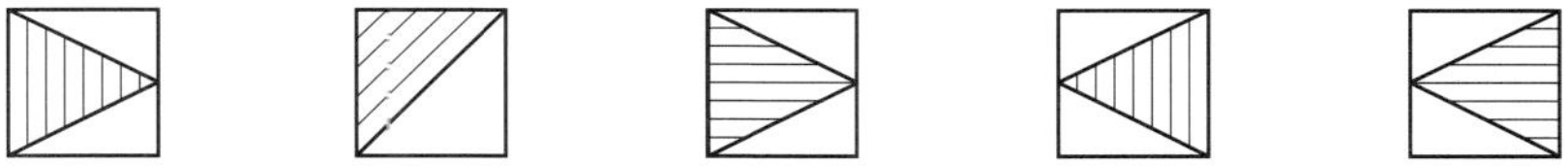

a b c d e

59

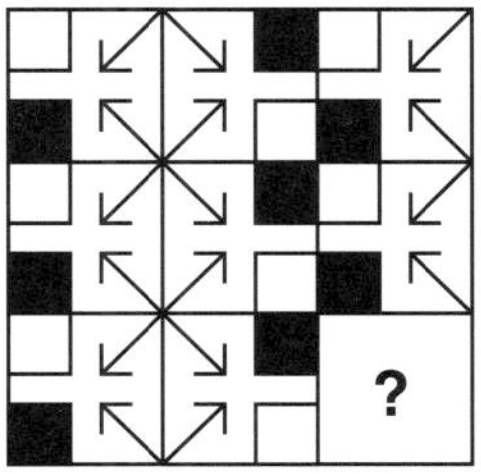

a b c d e

60

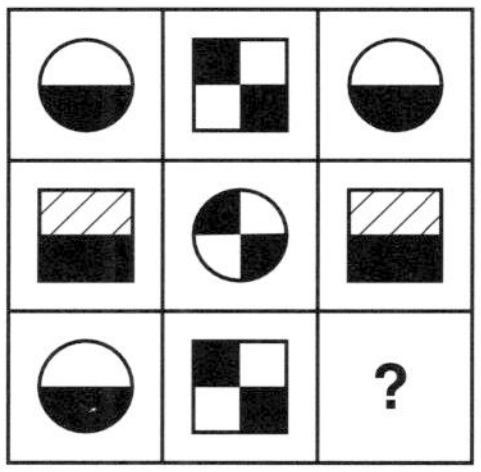

a b c d e

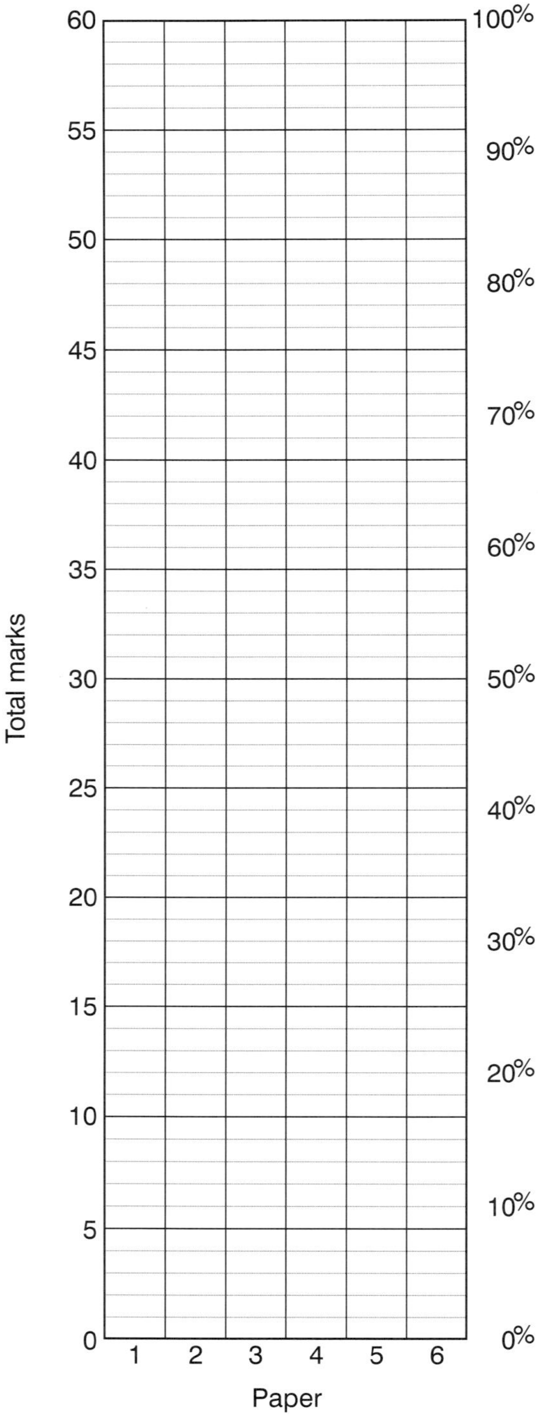
Total marks
60
55
50
45
40
35
30
25
20
15
10
5
0
100%
90%
80%
70%
60%
50%
40%
30%
20%
10%
0%
1
2
3
4
5
6
Paper